John Markowski

SEED, GROW, LOVE, WRITE

One man's unexpected and
slow journey to fulfillment

DANIELLE -

HOPE YOU ENJOY!

John M

Managing Editor: Katie Elzer-Peters
Copy Editor: Billie Brownell
Designer: Nathan Bauer

ISBN 13: 978-1548898151
ISBN 10: 1548898155

Printed in the United States of America

Mick and John
Thank you for holding me responsible.
Thank you for also offering up a safety net.
Thank you for never missing a thing.
Thank you for laughs.
Thank you for family.

CONTENTS

INTRODUCTION

"I need to find my passion."
"What is my purpose in life?"
"Who am I?"

How many people do you hear say this on a daily basis?
Have you said it yourself? I know I have.

But I've stopped.

While it wasn't easy, I found a way to remove these thoughts from my conscious brain. The unconscious brain is another story but we'll leave that for another day.

Here's how I did it:

I stopped waiting for my "aha" moment. Instead, I embrace the "hmmm" moments. They're not as loud and obvious, but they're more common and more real. I then looked back on my life and unearthed other "hmmm" moments. When I added them together, they revealed an "aha" epiphany.

I also now subscribe to the theory that our passions don't find us, we find them. We find them by living life, trying different things, embracing experiences, keeping our eyes open, managing the ebbs and flows, revisiting what we loved when we were young, and most importantly, just observing ourselves.

We don't have to jump out of a plane or hike the

Appalachian Trail.

We don't need a personal guru or hallucinogens.

We don't have to go all Elizabeth Gilbert and eat, pray, and love our way through life.

We make small discoveries and embrace those small joys. We take notes along the way. We quietly observe and feel. We become educated and we evolve.

Do all that and it can add up to so much more. And that "so much more" doesn't have to equate to monetary wealth or fame or anything else large in scale.

It can be as simple as slowly discovering a love for gardening, becoming immersed in that world, allowing that world to stoke creativity, which in turn pushed a former journalism major to rediscover the joys of writing, which in turn resulted in a book.

This book.

I wrote this book so I could finally write this book. I selfishly wrote this book to learn more about myself.

When I started I wasn't sure of the book's exact path. I had a few stories in mind and that was it. But then the keystrokes quickly piled up and so much unfolded right before my eyes. Memories I had forgotten were dredged up and for good reason: they easily fit the narrative. They helped me come to terms not only with who I am, but where I still want to go.

I want this book to be inspirational in a purposefully understated way. The world is obsessed right now with "finding out who we are" or "identifying our purpose in life" or "discovering our passion," and it can be stressful and frustrating when we put ourselves through this type of self-analysis. We can only handle so much Tony Robbins shtick before we want to give up and surrender to our normal and mundane lives.

But what if those answers are right in front of us and we're too blind to see them? What if we're striving for too much and too soon? What if we take a moment to reflect on our lives with a healthy and positive outlook? What if the answer is to remain patient and allow life to play itself out?

The series of stories that follow track my journey from childhood to current day. It's a sort of origin story and memoir. There's nothing salacious (sort of) and oftentimes the story seems small and insignificant on the surface, but upon further reflection there is an important lesson to be learned.

I hope this book helps you take a closer look at your own life so you might rediscover what it is that has energized you over the years. Maybe it's obvious or maybe it takes more introspection.

I hope it points you in an interesting direction.

I hope it speeds up your happiness by slowing you down.

I hope it encourages you to be okay with taking baby steps while still dreaming big.

I hope you dig it.

This is my story.

4

CHAPTER 1

WHO AM "I"?

I'm sure you're now thinking, *"Why should I listen to this guy?"* and *"Let me see his credentials."* Fair point, I'd ask the same thing. So here it is.

I'm a 45-year-old happily married man with a beautiful and quietly hysterical wife, two stellar children, and the world's greatest rescue mutt.

We live in the ideal-sized home for us in rural Hunterdon County, New Jersey.

My wife and I have worked in corporate America for 20-plus years each, and we have no complaints financially.

I continue to work at the same company that hired me in 1997. I have no intention of leaving anytime soon (key word being "soon").

Life is good.

But here's the rub: I found my complete self on the side. No, there hasn't been a midlife crisis. I never once considered quitting my job to pursue some crazy calling.

I discovered my love of gardening through pursuing what I loved doing when I was a child, failing badly in other areas, and good old curiosity.

That love eventually helped unearth a long-lost passion for writing.

It's as simple as that.

That's what makes me happy.

That's what makes me whole.

And here's the best part: I'm still smack dab in the middle of it. I dream of writing books professionally as a new career. I still fancy myself as a host of a gardening TV show.

But I'm in no rush, even in my mid-forties.

I'm allowing it all to play out one step at a time.

And now I want to get you there with me. I hope that by taking you all along for the ride as I relive some of the tales of my life, it will do something for you, unlock something you didn't know needed to be unlocked.

It doesn't have to be big.

Small can work. Small can make you infinitely happy. Small can build upon itself.

And if big is in the cards, that's the gravy on the mashed potatoes.

So won't you join me? I bet you can find your thing too.

We'll laugh a lot.

We'll cry a bit.

And I'll do my best to gently encourage you into examining your own life.

SEED

CHAPTER 2

FALLING LEAVES

*My father taught me to work; he did not teach
me to love it.*

— *Abraham Lincoln*

Every serious gardener I know seems to have an origin story.

"I grew up watching Grandma tend to her garden and together we used to watch the bees jump from flower to flower in search of pollen."

"I remember running through fields of wildflowers as a child and spending hours there, free as can be."

"My dad put a trowel in my hands when I was 2 years old."

"The taste of those plump, ripe tomatoes in summer never left me."

Me? I got nothing.

I've poured over the archival footage of my childhood and after hours of research I can confidently say there's nothing that stands out.

In fact, I'm disturbed by how singularly focused I was as a child. It was all sports, all the time. If I wasn't watching it on TV, I was in the backyard throwing a baseball into the tree branches above, trying to make diving catches like Fred Lynn.

The obsession I had with organizing my baseball cards is therapy worthy as you'll see in a future chapter.

I was studying the Las Vegas NFL point spreads and competing in football pools against my dad's fellow teachers before I had my multiplication tables memorized.

I convinced my fifth grade class to bet against our teacher, Mr. Isola, on Georgetown in the 1982 NCAA Basketball Championship game. We lost and had extra homework.

No signs of a future gardener.

But then I realized I was looking at it all wrong. It was a much more circuitous and subtle route, a series of connected events mixed with random occurrences that laid the groundwork first for my love of the outdoors (and when I say "outdoors," I mean the "yard" and not silly stuff like camping) and ultimately gardening.

I feel confident in saying that it all started with my father's obsession with getting rid of the fallen leaves each autumn.

I grew up on Oak Avenue, an aptly named street as our 1950s Cape Cod-style home sat underneath a canopy of gigantic oak trees. Those trees produced quite the bounty of leaves in fall as did the wandering leaves from neighbors' trees. Our backyard was one big leaf orgy.

Every Saturday in fall was dedicated to eradicating these leaves. And it was only on Saturdays.

Like the good Lord suggested, we rested on Sunday.

There were no exceptions. My family followed the letter of the religious law to a tee. I kept this family rule from my friends because I didn't want them to think we were Amish. It became easy to find an excuse why I couldn't go to McDonalds or the arcade. Staying indoors and watching TV was encouraged. It was weird but awesome.

In the early years, the leaves were removed through raking. We'd rake one section at a time onto a giant tarp and then drag that tarp to the front yard where the leaves were deposited over the front wall. The township would then pick them up on a weekly basis.

As technology advanced, we invested in a leaf blower and our job became much less labor intensive. The leaves could be blown onto the tarp and our forearms were spared. We'd still have to drag the tarp to the front wall, but the limited raking was a blessing.

It looked perfect outside each Saturday evening as we settled in, nursed our sore muscles, and watched *Solid Gold.*

But then more leaves would fall the next day and the days after; hence the need to do it again the following Saturday.

As a kid there was nothing I wanted to do less than tackle those leaves each weekend. I would pray for rain or pray something else would come up but those efforts were futile, and there we were again, Dad and I ankle deep in crispy brown leaves.

I remember one specific Saturday when I begged to be able to go to the high school football game with my friends but was told that my chores came first. What was this, *Little House on the Prairie*? None of my friends ever had to tend to chores. Why was I being punished? And while I'm at it, why weren't my sisters part of this leaf-removal enterprise?

At first I sulked and begrudgingly raked and raked.

This is stupid, more leaves are going to fall the minute we're done. Why don't we just wait until the last leaf has fallen and then take care of them all at once?

But then the sulking would slowly dissipate as I got lost in the odd joy of hard labor. I couldn't sustain my anger towards my dad. It almost pissed me off more that I was no longer pissed off. I was a sellout, not properly representing the disenfranchised class of forced child labor.

I learned to take extreme pride in our work. Even if it only lasted a day, I valued seeing that our efforts had paid off.

I loved the ache in my arms and legs post-shower on Saturday evening. I felt mature and useful and scoffed at my lazy friends who weren't getting the physical workout that I was.

I never held a grudge after my initial complaints. This was better than watching the high school football team lose by 35 points. This was a true sense of accomplishment.

Our father/son bonding, while often bound in silence out of exhaustion, was something I didn't appreciate enough at the time. It wasn't until my freshman year in college, when I was away at school during those leaf-raking months, that I realized how much I missed it and how badly I felt that I couldn't be there to help my dad.

Autumn was crisp and cool weather.

Autumn was football season.

Autumn was apples and pumpkins and Halloween.

But autumn was also raking leaves with my dad, consulting with him on NFL predictions, and together eating salt bagels loaded with butter.

Looking back on it now, the leaf management program kickstarted my deep appreciation of a well-kept yard. I didn't *help* in the yard as much as I, too, *owned* that yard.

That notion eventually extended to other "yard" tasks:

- cutting the lawn
- trimming the lawn
- using an edger-with-wheel contraption that created killer straight edges along our front sidewalk.

By the time I was in high school, I was our family landscaper. I didn't know the difference between an annual and a perennial. I couldn't identify a shrub by name. But I could trim the hell out of hedges. I could cut lines in the lawn like an artiste. Lawn edges were nothing but immaculate.

I carried over that notion to my first home many years later.

> *Chew on this:* What did you love to do as a child? Why are certain memories stronger than others? There's a kernel of inspiration in there if you look close enough.

CHAPTER 3

MULCH

One of the idiosyncrasies of the built American landscape is our fascination with mulch. It's in our yards and gardens; it is in the parking lots of our fast food chains and grocery stores; and it is in our airports and along our highways. We spread it everywhere. We spread it thickly.

—Thomas Rainer

Hey Johnnie Mulchowski, are you coming out with us tonight or what?

That was the running joke throughout high school. I do give you credit, Adam Blom, for the creative name, even if it infuriated 15-year-old me back in 1987. When you're an insecure teen who wants nothing more than the attention to be on someone else, you become overly sensitive to any name-calling.

But I digress…

I may be rewriting the Markowski family history book and if so, I'm sorry, Dad. For now, in the interest of completing this book, I'll go with my memory.

We discovered the wonder that is mulch in fall of 1986. I associate it with the New York Mets winning the World Series and the ball going through Buckner's legs. I also associate it with entering high school that same year.

One day I woke to a massive pile of something sitting on our driveway. My first thought was my dad had flipped his lid and ordered manure but that would have smelled much worse. I also knew it wasn't soil based on its texture.

I was stumped.

When I walked back through the front door on that fall morning and located my newspaper-reading father, I didn't even have to ask.

"That is mulch, my young and powerful son, and we will be laying it all down today. Mulch suppresses the weeds and looks fantastic and neat. We each will have our own wheelbarrow and the yard will look tremendous when we are done."

My initial thought: Leaf removal, lawn cutting, lawn trimming, and now mulch? Will the list of chores never end?

My second thought: Is this the new normal?

My third thought: Do I need to be taught the logistics of this thing you call "wheelbarrow"?

My fourth thought: What's the purpose of this mulch again?

My fifth thought: Hand me the sports section when you're done.

The memories that stick with you from childhood are funny. We had retaining walls along the front of our home. Because of that, we couldn't push the lawnmower or any other outdoor equipment directly from our street level garage to the front lawn. It required us to push it up the neighbor's long and steep driveway where we could then cut through the one opening within the seven-foot-high hedges that separated our properties.

I always thought of the neighbor's driveway as our driveway because we used it so often. I would hang out there with friends and not give it a second thought. My sisters would draw rainbows in chalk on their driveway.

I often wonder if they ever cared about our usage of their property. Did we sign an official contract or was it an implied neighborly agreement? My gut tells me an arrangement like this wouldn't fly today.

That first mulch installation experience, while labor intensive, was phenomenal. Not only because I was a natural with the wheelbarrow, capable of maneuvering in the tightest of spaces, but because I fell in love with its smell and its ability to transform the landscape.

We once again used the neighbor's driveway as our launching point to get the mulch-filled wheelbarrows to where they needed to go. We'd dump and run back for more, only taking a break to spread the stuff evenly in the garden beds. It was a great thigh and leg workout, especially if the mulch was wet from a recent rain.

I immediately wanted to take back my negative first impressions that, fortunately, I thought but never vocalized. Not too unlike my rush to judgment with leaf clean-up in fall.

I loved getting on my hands and knees and spreading it out equally. I loved spreading it in difficult to reach places. As my dad labeled it then, it was best to "hand spread" mulch rather than use a metal rake.

He was so right.

Mulching became a yearly event from that day forward. The Markowski Mulch was every June. My father would be sure to announce the date ahead of time to ensure my calendar was properly updated.

We mulched everything.

See that area where the grass refuses to grow? Mulch that shit, John.

Don't be afraid to mulch the driveway if need be.

So now I was not only a master of lawn cutting, lawn trimming, lawn edging, and leaf removal, but I was a master of laying down the mulch.

I truly owned the outdoors, or at least the outdoors directly surrounding my home.

I was Johnnie F'n Mulchowski.

As my father got older and I no longer lived at home, it became more of a struggle for him to take care of mulching on his own. For a time I was able to join him each June to assist with the mulching. But it became more and more difficult to coordinate so my father began paying a local landscaper to install the mulch.

The year before making the commitment to outsourcing the job, my dad dreamt up a brilliant marketing campaign in order to secure the help of the family for one last Markowski Mulch. He announced that there would be a "Mulch Party" on July 7, 2002. We would eat like kings after we all mulched like kings.

We all bought in and my brother-in-law and my sister's boyfriend assisted with the task. They were overwhelmed by the heat and humidity and the necessity to lay three inches of mulch. I ignored them. I distinctly remember them playing Rage Against the Machine on a boombox (yeah, I just said boombox) as a means of getting pumped to work and thinking, *"I don't need this. They are weak."*

We got it done.

I loved every second of it and have a clear memory of coming inside after we were done to see my very beautiful and very pregnant wife sitting on the couch directly under the window air conditioning unit. She was due in four weeks and we couldn't have been more excited.

Four days later her water broke, and my son, Jack, was born.

I still associate his three-weeks-early arrival with the Mulch Party.

One job was coming to an end, and one was only just beginning.

> ***Chew on this:*** I stopped using dyed mulch after learning of the harm it can cause to the soil. If we can find small ways to improve our lives, others' lives, and the planet on a daily basis, we'll make an effect over time. And we'll be happier for it.

CHAPTER 4

AZALEAS

If you ain't Dutch, you ain't much.

—Unknown

I grew up in Midland Park, New Jersey, a borough of 7,000 or so that is located in the northern part of the state (we NJ'ers identify as Northern, Central, or Southern). Those from northern New Jersey speak with a New York accent ("fuhgeddaboudit"), those from southern New Jersey speak with a Philly accent (the word "home" is pronounced as "hewm"), and those in the central part of the state can go either way. Yes, I'm painting with a broad brush here, but trust me, it's not too far off.

Midland Park had, and still has, a strong Dutch influence. Don't quote me here, but nearly 75 percent of the last names in town start with "Van," "VanDe," or "De." My mother's maiden name is Van Veen and I knew many VanDeVeens and DeVries.

While there wasn't a strong Dutch culinary influence in town and we didn't have many Dutch festivals or carnivals that I can recall, we did have a lot of Protestant "Reformed" churches, hard to decipher accents, and lots of oddly tall, blond people.

My grandfather's name was Martin Van Veen. He was born in Holland and came to the U.S. (Paterson, New Jersey) as a teenager. Soon after arriving, he met my Iowan grandmother, also Dutch, whose last name was Jeffer, and settled in Midland Park. My mother and her two siblings were raised in the same house my grandparents lived in for 60-plus years before they both passed away in the early 2000s.

My grandfather worked as a house painter and hustled by taking on odd jobs here and there. He had an immigrant's work ethic and was very stingy with his money. He also dabbled in taxidermy, which weirded me out as a kid. I wish I had asked him more questions about that before he passed.

My grandfather could make you laugh to the point of tears, but it had little to do with his sense of humor. He loved to tell jokes but it was never the punchline that gave you the giggles. He was unable to finish a joke because he laughed his way through the entire punchline. We never really knew what the punchline was, and it didn't matter because his tear-filled laughter was so infectious that you couldn't do anything but laugh along with him.

We were a close-knit family growing up with many holidays spent at my grandparents' home. Six boy cousins, all within five years of age, meant serious sports competition. There were intense Wiffle ball games and street hockey often ended with fisticuffs. We held competitive horseshoes tournaments. Every get-together culminated with a game of Kick the Can as the darkness descended upon us. Even our younger female siblings were allowed to play.

My grandmother was an incredible cook and baker and she always provided a feast during these festivities. She was loving in a quirky way and had an incredible sense of humor. Whenever we left her house, she would remove her false teeth and chase us into the car making the funniest and scariest face you've ever seen. We giggled and shat our pants at the same time.

Since my immediate family grew up in the same town as my grandparents, we were often at their house other than during the holidays. "Coffee" after church on Sunday was a personal favorite. When I reached the eighth grade I was allowed to forego Sunday School for good and was permitted to join the adults. I soaked in the family and church gossip while eating windmill cookies and drinking Pathmark Half and Half soda. My younger sisters had to suffer through singing hymns and awkward Bible lessons back at church. Ha to them.

When I was old enough to take the two-mile bike ride to school, I would occasionally stop at my grandparents' house before heading home after school ended. They would give me a Fudgsicle and we'd sit on their back porch. I'd fill them in on what was going on in school. I would lie about how much I loved it.

Our conversations inevitably ended with a trip into the backyard where we'd tour my grandfather's garden. It was always immaculate—no weeds and perfect bed lines. That always appealed to my aesthetic and my love of order; I never thought of it as a "garden" but as a "landscape."

I remember taking it as a challenge to see if we could make our yard look as neat and organized as his. I turned grass trimming into an art form. It was suburbia "gardening" at its best, even if it only involved a Lawnboy push mower and a string trimmer.

My favorite part of my grandfather's yard was the sweeping path that ran from their back patio, underneath the clothesline filled with my grandfather's sleeveless undershirts, past the perfectly manicured rose bushes, and ending at one end of the garden beds where he seemed to have collected hundreds of azaleas. The path was made up of irregularly shaped slate slabs that were evenly spaced within the impossibly green lawn. I liked to challenge myself to see if I could jump from one to the next without ever touching the lawn.

But those azaleas.

OMFG.

They were gigantic and almost impossible to look at when in bloom. The flower colors were blinding with every color imaginable included. There wasn't green to be found anywhere; they were inundated with blooms. Come to think of it, all of Midland Park was overrun with azaleas each and every May. Was that a Dutch thing? An '80s thing? A suburban thing?

Hmm.

I couldn't have told you the name of one other plant in his garden back then even though he identified each for me every time we toured the garden together.

But I sure as hell knew what an azalea was.

His smile and passion wouldn't let me forget it.

My grandfather was so proud of his azaleas and that pride made me smile even as a self-involved and easily distracted teenager.

What I wouldn't give to jump into a time machine and travel back to that path in 1981. I'd pick his brain over ten Fudgsicles. I'd bring a notebook and write down every tip he had on how to grow the perfect rose. I'd mimic his rose pruning techniques. I only acknowledged his flawless roses through photographs after it was too late. They somehow escaped me as a kid.

Oh! how I wish I'd had the knowledge back then that gardening would become such an enormous part of my future. I'd be kicking even more ass today.

I wish I had taken even a branch of one of his azaleas before we cleared out their house after it was sold.

I wish I had photographed that path.

I wish I fought harder to get that cool bird feeder.

I wish I grabbed a few tools and displayed them creatively in my own garden.

But I'm thrilled that a few of those stepping stones line a path in my garden today. I treat them with kid gloves because they provide that link I never want to break.

Chew on this: Talk to friends and family about your aspirations. They are the people who have your best interests in mind. Your inner circle is the perfect sounding board.

CHAPTER 5

THE LEAF REPORT

*Education is what remains after one has
forgotten what one has learned in school.*

—Albert Einstein

When we eventually master time travel, I'm going to return to 1986, September 3, 1986, to be exact. That was the first day of my freshman year at Midland Park High School.

That was the year we ninth graders from MP merged with students from the nearby town of Ho-Ho-Kus, New Jersey. That was the year it took me 45 minutes too long to get ready for school each morning. That was the year when the family had to take out a loan to pay for my Clearasil pad addiction. That was the year I forced myself to listen to REM because I thought that would give me school hallway cred. That's what the cool kids were playing on their Walkmans.

That was also the year Adam Blom and I bonded in shared self-consciousness and enormous growth spurts. We were friends before then, but freshman year sealed our friendship for life.

We were dorks and we knew it. Not the type of nerds who are endearing in pop culture now; we didn't play Dungeons & Dragons or anything like that. We were just awkwardly tall and shy and braces-faced boys.

I was 6 foot 3 by this point; Adam was almost 6 foot 6. Our clothes never quite fit right because we were growing at such a rapid pace. There also wasn't a muscle to be found on either of our bodies.

We were consumed by girls but couldn't talk to them. We chatted on the phone all night, every night, dreaming of upping our coolness or at least gaining the nerve to step out of our collective shells.

That's why I want to go back in time and chat with my 14-year-old self. I want to tell me to relax and realize everyone else is in the same boat. Everyone has anxiety about fitting in. Nobody knows who they are yet. High school ultimately doesn't matter. To have made a friend for a lifetime and to still stay in touch with that friend even though we live 1,000 miles apart is a win.

Just be comfortable in your skinny skin and your too-short Levis.

The one thing we did have was a sense of humor. We made each other laugh with ease. If we were on a comedic rant, we had all of the confidence in the world.

We ruled the world of self-deprecation. Getting people to laugh lessened our anxieties. And there is nothing people like more than self-mocking. It relaxes and disarms them and does them well to know someone else feels the same way.

Adam is still the funniest person on this planet. Case in point: He and his brother were fighting over who would have to sacrifice an extra slice of pizza after we did the pizza math.

Eight slices meant two of us would have three slices, and one of us would have two. After a nasty back and forth Adam solved it all by smashing the entire pie into his own face.

It was Jim Carrey before Jim Carrey existed. It was genius and true dedication to the comedic craft.

Adam and I were in the same biology class that year. Mr. Hoitsma was our teacher, and he was the coolest and most chill teacher in our high school. His demeanor never changed; he was soft-spoken and patient and handled the "bad" kids with ease. Actually his calm demeanor prevented students from goofing off at all, which I remember realizing even then was a killer strategy.

Adam had a way of making me laugh during biology even when he sat across the room from me. I would glance over and he would be making a goofy face, anticipating my look. He would curse out loud during class but did so in a way where it was muffled by other sounds. If Adam was talking to another student, he could artfully mock them without them realizing it. He was a genius performer.

In spring of '87, Mr. Hoitsma gave us an assignment that at first appeared to be painfully boring. It was entitled "The Leaf Report." It was an annual project that Mr. Hoitsma assigned in every one of his biology classes dating back to when my mother had him in the mid-1960s. Yes, I grew up in that kind of small town.

The gist of the report was: Identify twenty different

trees or shrubs, include a leaf from each, and provide a corresponding write-up.

There were bonuses available with this report and that's what pushed the report from "must-do for class" to "I still remember the report to this day." Bonus points could be attained if we located "rare" trees and shrubs and included them within our report.

Game on.

To the shock of no one, Adam and I worked on our report together.

We walked the entire town in our quest to find our trees and shrubs. It was a cliché coming-of-age moment. It was our version of *Stand by Me* minus the dead body and terrifying local gang.

Finishing the required section of the report was easy. We got that out of the way early so we could focus on the more interesting task of finding the "rare" items.

We had no clue how to identify and locate a rare tree or shrub so it forced us to make judgment calls along the way. If it looked unusual, we looked it up in our handy reference books and then cross-checked to see if it qualified as rare.

We found a big leaf magnolia tree right around the corner from my house. I had walked by that tree hundreds of times before and never gave it a second glance. I'm still not sure just how rare it was, but we were giddy with bonus points.

We ventured to my great aunt's house and her endless acres of woods. If I remember correctly, we found at least three rare plants on her property. I want to say there was a *Cryptomeria* and a rare bleeding heart. (I am correct; I just confirmed with Adam via text.)

I remember running into wild animals that apparently had escaped from the wildlife center that bordered her property. Or maybe that has been fabricated over the years. (Yes, I lied; Adam confirmed this via text as well.)

We worked on the report for weeks and were actually sad when it was all done. Learning was freaking fun. I never looked at a tree or shrub the same from that point forward; I was always curious as to its name and its rareness.

The report gave us an excuse to not talk about girls or what parties were coming up. It was an escape and a learning experience held outside of the classroom.

I often wonder how much that assignment initiated my love of plants. While it was more than a decade later before I planted a shrub in my own garden, there has to be a reason why I still have such a vivid memory of that project. It had to have kicked something into motion.

I will forever be indebted to Mr. Hoitsma for that. But I will remain forever pissed off at him as well. I only got a B+ on the report because I spelled "deciduous" wrong five times.

I was livid then, and I'm livid now.

I found that report and the grade explanation a few years ago as my parents were moving out of my childhood home. I actually shared it with Mr. Hoitsma through Facebook.

I was still looking for his rationale to this day, although with tongue firmly planted in cheek. Couldn't it have been -1 instead of -5 since it was the same word misspelled all five times?

I've heard nothing to date.

Chew on this: Is there a school assignment or work project that you fondly remember to this day? Why do you think it still resonates all these years later?

CHAPTER 6

BASEBALL CARDS

For every minute spent organizing, an hour is earned.

—Benjamin Franklin

I was **not** the kid who had to be told to clean his room.

I was **not** the kid who had to be told to put his toys away.

I was the kid who enjoyed running the vacuum in his room on a weekly basis.

I was the kid who dusted his own furniture and periodically cleaned out all of his dresser drawers.

I was a neat, tidy, and organized little lad and that made me a fairly easy child to manage.

I was the kid who kept his shit organized, especially his baseball cards.

Oh, those baseball cards.

I still get nostalgic shivers of joy when I think back to those beautiful card designs from back in the day, of the gorgeous action shots of the players donning their killer wares. The unforgettable '70s mustaches and '80s perms preserved on cardboard for eternity.

From the backs of these cards, I still remember useless player facts like their place of birth. I knew where most played in the minor leagues before they even sniffed making it to the major leagues. I could tell you how many home runs a utility player on the Minnesota Twins hit in 1982.

It was an obsession.

Baseball cards ruled my life from the late '70s through the '80s and into the early '90s. I preferred sorting my cards to doing just about anything else during that time.

Introverted? Yes.

Nerdy sports kid? Yes.

Regret a minute of it? Hell to the no.

I would sort cards by a player's last name, or by card number, or by dollar value. I would make lists of the cards I needed to complete a set. I would closely monitor the box scores of Major League Baseball games and rank my cards by who was playing well and who was on a cold streak. I would write down the book value of cards and continue to monitor them so I could appropriately sell high or buy low.

I had binders upon binders filled with the more valuable cards, secured in plastic sheets. I would buy, trade, and gamble (yes, gamble) as many cards of a potential superstar as I could. I'd have six pages of Barry Bonds rookie cards and happily stare at my investment for hours on end. While everyone else was playing Atari or watching *Diff'rent Strokes*, I was quietly building a mini empire within the four walls of my immaculately clean and organized bedroom.

I often imagine how insanely cool it would have been to have access to Microsoft Excel or some other spreadsheet software back in those card-collecting days. I would've spent months on end logging my entire card collection into the spreadsheet. I could then sort however the hell I wanted, whenever the hell I wanted. I could've run reports daily to assess my profits and expenses. I could've hired a team and been a cool young boss.

I would've really never left my bedroom.

At its peak value, I had cards that could pay six month's rent for a New York City apartment. I had visions of them continuing to ascend in value for perpetuity and someday funding a lifestyle where I'd never have to work.

Then the baseball card market crashed, and my 37 Barry Bonds rookies were worthless. The majority of my cards were worthless. They all now reside in my basement and I debate throwing them out on a weekly basis.

All the time and effort put into curating my collection feels worthless. I should've sold most of the cards when I had the opportunity to make good money, but I naively believed they could only ever go *up* in value.

I was crushed.

This is the part where I'm supposed to tell you that I took all of the business lessons learned from this time and applied it elsewhere in my life. The laws of supply and demand or how to properly price a commodity were clearly a part of baseball card collecting. And there was a need to develop negotiation skills at a young age when attempting to sell a card to a greedy dealer.

Not too long ago, I would have told you that "no," I never extended these skills to another venture in my life.

I never took an economics class in college. I've never had a job in sales in my life. My best attempts at negotiation are trying to get my kids to go to bed at a decent hour. I've lost every single time.

But once my son became obsessed with card collecting, I got the itch to get back in. He, too, started with collecting for collecting's sake. He had favorite players and loved opening boxes of cards. I could watch him for days, easily falling back into the joys of the hobby that once ruled my life.

As he got older and wiser and discovered eBay and YouTube, he left the "hobby" behind and became a mini-mogul in the world of sports cards. Short printings of cards have become the norm in the industry and that scarcity has driven the price of cards into hundreds and even thousands of dollars.

My son has finagled his way into some ridiculously valuable cards. Christmas has been an endless parade of card boxes. He has collected players' autographs through the mail and in person. Packages come and go on a daily basis.

He's making money and reinvesting it into other cards.

We bond like mad over it. I feel a rush as he gives me his strategy. I listen to all that he has to say because his research is sound.

And then it hit me. I had my shot at retribution.

I could get back into what I loved doing as a kid. Isn't that what the self-help gurus prescribe? Take that passion from childhood and find a way to reinvent it back into your life? And maybe, just maybe, make some decent coin this time?

I'm back in.

I've bought and sold cards for profit.

It's fun.

I'm energized.

Card collecting requires tracking of card values daily, or tracking a player's "stock," which keeps it forever entertaining and exciting with a dash of gambling for extra spice. I pay attention to baseball stats once again.

But it isn't all about turning a profit. I still get a palpable feeling of excitement from a well-designed card coupled with the perfect action shot. It doesn't matter that the subjects aren't much older than my son. It's still in my blood.

I have a weird fascination with 1977 Topps baseball cards. They're groovy and nostalgic, and if you look deeper, like I have, there are endlessly fascinating stories about the players in that set. I've written articles about these specific cards and published them online. They were the easiest stories I've ever written. A super niche topic but super fun; don't be shocked to see a future book on it.

But most important, the card collecting has become a father/son thing with the son acting as the mentor. He's as smart as a whip and isn't afraid to call me out when I'm wrong.

I'm cool with that.

Beyond rediscovering a passion from my younger

days, I've also found another way to love me some more organization. All of my purchases and sales are carefully logged in a spreadsheet. I'm constantly tweaking it and analyzing it. It's the modern-day version of making lists on index cards.

Being organized is a necessity for me.

I can't function if my world is disorganized.

It alleviates stress and provides a great sense of control.

That is who I am, for better or worse.

> ***Chew on this:*** Don't be afraid to dive into what you love no matter how childish it may seem.

CHAPTER 7

THE POWER OF THE VACUUM

I'm not going to vacuum until Sears makes one you can ride on.

—Roseanne Barr

I love to procrastinate. I'm an out and proud procrastinator. It's been in my blood since the day I was born.

So many people take issue with their own procrastination and vow to overcome their propensity to delay, delay, delay.

I embrace it. I've never tried to defeat it.

I use it to my advantage.

I was the wait-until-the-last-minute-to-study student. It was always the night before a big test that I'd finally open my textbook. And the studying would commence late that evening. While the house was asleep, I was just getting started.

I needed the pressure in order to focus. I needed to allow panic to set in before I could get my brain to do its thing. I didn't fear late nights and I didn't fear last second studying as I walked into the classroom to take the test the next morning. The pressure brought out my best.

One of my go-to moves the night before a big test was first to vacuum and organize my bedroom, a classic delay tactic of the procrastinator. But I wasn't just looking to push off the inevitable, I did this strategically:

A clean room meant I had no need to worry about a clean room.

A clean room provided a relaxing atmosphere in which to thrive academically.

But most importantly, a clean room meant momentum. It was a feeling of accomplishment that fed my need for more accomplishment. Seeing those heavenly vacuum lines in the carpet was my gateway to more "doing." Removing the Smarties wrappers and sock fuzz from the rug was invigorating and inspired me to dive into the table of periodic elements.

I don't think it's an exaggeration to say that the vacuum helped me get through high school.

I'm still riding the theory of vacuum momentum to this day.

My wife isn't allowed to touch the Dyson. That's my job and my job only. She knows this and accepts it. Everyone stays out of my way when I get going.

I've fine-tuned my vacuuming technique over the years and I'm simply the best there is. If there ever were to be a Vacuuming Olympics, I'd kill in the trials and make my hometown proud.

I can maneuver the Dyson around obstacles, like the

dog or kids eating breakfast, without skipping a beat. I can get those mysterious webs on the ceiling and the microscopic bugs hiding under the floor moldings in one fell swoop. I can create designs in the carpet like Bob Ross.

But not unlike that amateur student residing in his red, white, and blue striped wallpapered bedroom adorned with posters of Darryl Strawberry back in 1985, I still use vacuuming as a launching pad. I still use it for momentum. I still use that sense of accomplishment to feed whatever needs to be done next.

Is it time to replace the gutters on the house? Vacuum first.

Is it time to do my taxes on April 14? Vacuum first.

Do we need to put together a vacation game plan? Vroom Vroom.

It's as if the vacuum sucks up all other distractions and allows me to focus on the tasks at hand. Once that motor starts running and once the dust starts to pile up inside the see-through canister, it's game on.

When managing a large garden like the one I'm still trying to tame to this day, there's never a shortage of things to do. I could dedicate a week straight to its upkeep and I'd still barely make a dent in the to-do list. It's just short of brutally overwhelming.

And shockingly, I'm also a procrastinating gardener. I'm good at building a plan and mapping out what needs to be done and by when, but I'm lousy with the execution.

I know those weeds need to be pulled before they set seed and triple in size; I just can't bring myself to be proactive and eradicate them when it most makes sense. I need to know the situation is dire before I jump into action.

And when dire arrives, the first thing I do is cut the lawn.

Lawn cutting = vacuuming.

I use it in the same way as vacuuming; to gather momentum. Even if I think of the lawn as a lower priority compared to the garden, I still like the look (and aroma) of a freshly cut lawn. It feels good to step off the tractor and scan the sea of unified green.

The practice of accomplishment-building applies both indoors and outdoors.

Now that the grass looks nice and neat, wouldn't the entire landscape look better if I now removed those weeds?

And while I'm at it, I should finish shaping that bed line.

And I should divide the irises and replant the new divisions in that empty section of garden near the garage.

Ride the wave, John, ride the wave. Make this garden shine.

> ***Chew on this:*** Figure out what kicks your ass into gear. For me it's a vacuum. What is it for you?

CHAPTER 8

FRIEND OR FOE?

*Friend: one attached to another by
affection or esteem.*

—Merriam-Webster Dictionary

How many of you have or had a "friend" who didn't necessarily meet this definition? Where the friendship wasn't really based on "affection" or "esteem"?

All of you? Good to know.

I'll call him Zeke.

Zeke and I met in eighth grade when he moved to my hometown. We instantly bonded over our love of sports, specifically our mutual love of playing basketball. We played on the same rec team where I was more of a forward since I was taller, and he was the point guard because he was a solid ball handler.

Zeke pushed off illegally every time we played one-on-one and it so pissed me off. The angrier I got, the more he enjoyed playing. He lived to get me riled up.

Zeke and I weren't necessarily "friends" as much as we were competitive acquaintances who spent a lot of time together pushing each other's buttons. I'm not sure how that type of relationship is defined.

Zeke loved busting on me every chance he got. And he

never cared if I gave it right back to him. He cherished the times when I got angry or annoyed because it wasn't in my nature. I said nasty things to him that I've never said to anyone else, and he never took offense.

Zeke was and still is a very handsome man. All of the ladies in school had a crush on him. No matter how poorly he treated them, they came back for more. It was sad to observe in real time.

Because Zeke and I were tight, I became the default wing man. And by "wing man" I mean all of the girls came crying to me when he turned them down or blew them off. At first I enjoyed the attention from the ladies. I had negative-zero game so any interaction was okay with me. This, too, was sad to observe in real time.

The act grew old over time and I quickly realized this wasn't a good mate-finding strategy. This wasn't even a case of being in the "friend zone." This was me acting as Zeke's assistant and PR rep except I didn't get paid and I wasn't able to use the job as a springboard to something bigger and better.

Now, truth be told, I may have been using Zeke in my own right as well. I had a crush on his younger sister. I would throw up out of nervousness every time I tried to talk to her. But being at Zeke's house gave me unique access to one day—hopefully—not poop myself and actually have a real conversation with her outside of the public eye.

Then Zeke got wind of my crush. And he destroyed me with it. If she and I were ever in the same room and he witnessed it, he was relentless. The mocking never stopped, and I turned to mush each time. Yet I came back for more each time. I guess I assumed he would eventually relent but that didn't happen.

The embarrassment didn't end there. He "pantsed" me (pulled down my shorts and boxers) in front of his family while they were eating dinner. All was on display as they scarfed down their spaghetti. I can vouch for it being spaghetti because you remember weird details during those traumatic moments.

Zeke and I played Wiffle Ball on a daily basis during the summer. It was so competitive that I once threw the bat at him without care for his well-being. Of course, it was just a plastic bat so I wasn't that savage. Still, it was further proof that he could easily bring out the worst in me.

While we battled playing fake baseball, our mutual friend, Adam, whom you met earlier, would do anything to get our attention. He would run around in nothing but his underwear and steal the bat. It sounds hilarious and it was, but Zeke and I were so consumed with our own battles that we ignored him. If only I had recorded it at least once; YouTube would blow up.

I hope I've properly set things up, because I'm now ready to get to my point.

It's junior year in high school, the spring of 1989, and we were given an assignment in U.S. history to portray a historic figure from the past. It not only required a presentation but we also had to at least attempt to dress up like the people we were representing. Once the assignment was given, I had a knot in my stomach. Not only did I despise public speaking but to do so in costume would destroy me.

I had legendarily embarrassed myself during a pep rally for our basketball team only weeks prior, and I wasn't close to recovery. The pep rally host had handed me the microphone to say a few words about our upcoming game. I choked. I mumbled a few unintelligible words and handed the mic back. There was absolute silence, hundreds of uncomfortable faces, and the attempt to fire up the crowd backfired. Looking back, if I had just shouted "Let's kick Waldwick's ass" I could've escaped all of the self-hate. Oh well.

Zeke and I were to work together on this assignment. I don't remember if we volunteered to work together or if we were told to team up. My best guess is that I jumped at the chance to have someone else up there with me and since it was him, all eyes would not be on me.

We decided to be Laurel and Hardy because, why wouldn't I up the embarrassment level to 11? I was Hardy, and I clearly remember stuffing a pillow in my shirt and wearing a bowler hat. We worked on the project together at my house and Zeke hit on my younger sister. She loved it, so you can imagine how fun it was to witness it live. Zeke would grin at me as if to say, *"Look how easily I pulled that off."*

When the day arrived to present I couldn't walk or breathe. While we were prepared and nailed the assignment from an information perspective, I looked ridiculous and assumed I'd pass out after 15 seconds in front of the class.

But I killed it.

My competitive juices kicked in when I least expected it. I was all in and looking to own the stage like a well-seasoned stand-up comedian. The class howled at my impression. The class loved my mocking of Laurel. Zeke would not upstage me on this day.

Ms. Parente, our teacher, couldn't take her eyes off me. I still remember her look of shock and genuine appreciation of my out-of-nowhere performance. I probably could've asked her out then and there and she would have said "yes." That would have been awesome—and controversial.

I had such a rush afterwards. I enjoyed performing. I enjoyed not being me for those 15 minutes. It made up for the pep rally gaffe and then some. I was forced out of my shell and I was thankful for it.

Even after that successful moment, I still didn't sign up for the drama club.

I still sweated out each and every oral report from that point forward.

No one could convince me to talk at the next pep rally.

But I came to appreciate life forcing me into uncomfortable situations. I'd hate it all up until the moment when I had to perform and then, more often than not, I pulled it off.

That performer lives inside me to this day. It just needs

to be pulled out from an outside force.

Writing does that for me. I can be free with my words and honest without hesitation. I want to make people laugh and I want to elicit every emotion on the spectrum. I cherish putting that bowler hat back on and leaving myself for stretches.

Zeke brought a lot of that out of me, and for that, I guess I'm forever grateful.

Postscript

Zeke and I remained "friends" throughout the remainder of high school. We shared a limo at our senior prom and comforted each other at the Jersey Shore the next day after we had a miserable time with our dates.

Zeke "hooked up" with one of my family members at my wedding. And gave that same grin the next morning, which made me want to punch his teeth in.

Zeke and I have lost touch over the years.

I never made it to his wedding and I don't remember why.

We briefly reunited at his father's funeral.

I last saw him at another friend's wedding ten years ago.

I peek in on his family through his wife's Facebook account.

He sent me a text with a picture of he and my sister standing too close together after a chance encounter at the Jersey Shore. He still enjoyed tormenting me with sister nonsense.

I wouldn't mind smacking him again one day soon. And I'd kill to play him in Wiffle Ball.

Chew on this: Do you feel uninspired and stuck? It may be due to the people with whom you surround yourself. Try to get out of your comfort zone.

CHAPTER 9

CRIMINALLY IMPATIENT

Safe is death.

—John Tortorella

"When you graduate, please be aware that you will more than likely start out as an obituary writer for a local newspaper."

That one statement completely changed the course of my professional life. It pushed me to change my college major from journalism to criminal justice. It made me question the legitimacy of a college education. It confused me. It pissed me off.

Looking back on it now, I should've used it as fuel or motivation to prove my Journalism 101 professor wrong. I should've understood the purpose behind him making such a declaration. I should've stayed the course and persevered.

But I did none of those things.

I entered college in the fall of 1990 as a journalism major with dreams of someday writing for *Sports Illustrated* or a well-known—don't laugh—newspaper. In high school I had written for the school paper, had taken multiple journalism classes, and had written features on school coaches for various publications.

I may have been introverted, but I had no fear sharing my thoughts through writing.

My father still gushes about the essay I wrote for my college applications. In it, I was brutally honest about my inability to identify what I wanted to do with my life. I sold myself as well read and well-rounded with the hope that further schooling and experience would help me find my path. I still wonder if anyone ever read that essay and if it had any impact on the decision-making process. Probably not, but at least my dad was impressed. That means more.

During the first semester of my freshman year at Trenton State College (TSC), I wrote a few terrible stories for our school newspaper, *The Signal*. I remember one was a profile of the defunct women's gymnastics team. Another covered an upcoming archeology exhibit that was coming to the student center.

This was hard-hitting journalism at its finest.

When my professor dropped the quote that kicked off this story, it was right before the end of the first semester. It immediately threw me into a state of panic. I don't know if he intended it as inspiration, a reality check, or a little of both, but it made me reconsider my choice of supposed career path immediately.

By the end of freshman year, I was a practicing criminal justice major believing that gave me the best chance to get a "real" job after graduation. I abandoned my passion without a moment of reflection in favor of what I deemed to be a safer and smarter path.

I eventually added a minor in psychology because I had visions of becoming the next Jodie Foster after watching *Silence of the Lambs*. That's the kind of decision-making you get from a 19-year-old. A movie can sway your potential career choice. We should all be attending college when we're like, 30, after we've lived a little. How do I initiate this movement?

I visited prisons as part of the criminal justice curriculum. During one of those visits I was heckled by an inmate who kept repeating "Johnnie Markowski" over and over again. I eventually caved, turned around and realized the heckler was someone I had met at a prior job. Hector began to tell me what he did that lead to his incarceration, but the guards quickly intervened. I was kind of a rock star after that.

I sat in on emotional meetings in a home for wayward boys or whatever it was called back then. That was uncomfortable, awkward, and rewarding in an uncomfortably awkward way.

I participated in multiple "ride-alongs" with local police officers. On more than occasion I was told to keep the doors locked and to be ready to duck if necessary. That was fun.

I interned with the public defender's office in Trenton, New Jersey. My main responsibility was to conduct initial inmate interviews where I listened to 95 percent lies. My boss once attacked an inmate, and I had to step in between them. Ray was a tough and fearless SOB and I was not. I've forgotten how that altercation worked itself out and if Ray was okay.

I never took another class that required any writing. It was all practical, all the time.

I took the LSAT (Law School Admission Test) and scored decently. I have no memory of studying and no memory of when or where I took the test. But at least it kept my parents and their concern for my future at bay.

I applied to Seton Hall Law School and was added to their waiting list. I never pursued it from there. I had no burning desire to be a lawyer.

My first official job post-college was working for a private investigator. The first task I was given to complete on my own was to drop a summons on a rich dude who had given an STD to a woman he met while on vacation in Florida. There were guard dogs roaming the grounds of his estate behind what appeared to be a flimsy fence. I rang the doorbell and ran like hell and falsely claimed to have attempted to deliver the summons. If that was illegal, I'm sorry. I have no doubt that the dogs intended to kill me.

After three bizarre months of assisting undercover agents with this P.I. and getting paid very little, I secured a job with an insurance company hoping to move into their fraud department eventually. But first I had to learn everything there was to know about automobile claims.

The job was not fun. I got screamed at, deservedly so, a lot. We tried to nickel and dime every claimant, and they were vocal about their unhappiness. There were threats and surprise visits at our office. It was a great learning experience looking back, but it felt anything but that at the time.

I left after two years and went to another insurance company where I've now been for 21-plus years.

I feel just as lost running through my history post-journalism dream now as I did then.

As unhappy as I have been from time to time with these jobs, I continued to ignore writing. I forgot to miss it. Excuse the obvious pun, but that chapter had been written and it was buried in the deep recesses of my mind. I looked at myself as a naïve idealist who falsely believed that a career in writing was a possibility. I required a steady and secure job with benefits so I could provide for a family and build up a decent retirement fund. Writing would not provide that.

Why I didn't consider writing at night or "on the side" until years later is still beyond me. Maybe the advent of the internet, email, and blogs stirred it up (that's called foreshadowing). Before then few writing outlets existed.

While I have regrets, I still live by the mantra of better late than never.

> ***Chew on this:*** Is there something you gave up on too soon? Do you remember why? It's never too late to revisit it again.

CHAPTER 10

MAILMAN

Wearing shorts is a huge perk. I think it's probably one of the reasons people become mailmen. You also get to drive in that vehicle that should be illegal in the United States, where the steering wheel is on the other side. They have no rules! They are the punk rock of government jobs.

— Jimmy Fallon

I enjoy nothing more than oversharing with people I don't know very well. I love watching their reactions as I recount stories where I don't necessarily come out looking so great. I get a weird thrill portraying myself not in the greatest light. I have this need to humanize myself almost immediately upon meeting someone because I want to get the same thing in return.

I want back-and-forth authenticity.

When I tell these stories I like to think I'm slowly revealing details like a well-written thriller. I like to include strange details even if they don't feed the plot; they add texture and additional layers.

When I'm in storytelling mode, there is no timeframe referenced more than the one summer I was a mailman. Every day seemed to be an event. There was so much to observe, and all of my senses were at their highest because

I didn't have to think much when delivering mail.

It was a people watcher's dream.

I made immediate friends.

Three different ladies made me cookies.

I received a $2 bill as a gift on more than one occasion.

I felt alive and a bond with the people of the town.

I embodied the mailman stereotype (sans the uniform) you see on Sesame Street or in children's books.

"Good morning, John. Beautiful day isn't it?"

"It sure is, Carl. That lawn is filling in beautifully. Don't spend this Social Security check all at once, ha ha."

I miss it terribly.

I wish I'd considered the joys of people interaction when I pursued employment post-college. I wish I'd started a blog that summer even though the internet didn't exist yet. I wish I'd put myself in a position to have as many "interesting experiences" as humanly possible when I was still young.

I was a mailman for one summer back in 1992. This was between my sophomore and junior years in college.

I had more interesting experiences in those three months than I've had with all of my other jobs combined to date.

That's sad, isn't it?

To this day, it's the only non-desk job I've ever had. Damn, I wish I could go back and change that.

I was 20 years old that summer and I didn't have to be at work until 10 a.m. each morning. It was ideal for a lazy college student. I didn't even have to sort my mail. I just showed up, jumped in my truck, and was on my way.

This wasn't a drive to each mailbox and deliver situation. I walked the entire route, parking strategically along the way. I knew where I could walk across a lawn and where I couldn't due to a lawn-loving homeowner.

I still remember how I had to hold the mail for the greatest efficiency. Larger mail (magazines, flyers, and so forth) was cradled in my left arm against my bicep and letters were held in the left hand. My right hand was then used to pull from both stacks for each address.

I remember there were a lot of cicadas that summer.

I remember the joys of driving from the passenger seat, and I had not even one minor accident.

I remember hating mail slots built into front doors. They were a hassle to maneuver.

I still remember the exact address of the woman who received five to ten packages each and every day from QVC. I remember the guy who received multiple magazines a week fully covered in brown paper. I so wanted to peak in to read the titles, but I didn't want to risk a federal offense.

I wish I could have interviewed them both—no judgment, just mail carrier curiosity.

Those were all great memories but the following were by far the top highlights/lowlights from that magical summer of traversing the streets of suburban Glen Rock, New Jersey, with a giant satchel hanging over my left shoulder.

Naked guy

I saw all he had to offer as he descended the stairs that sunny morning. This happened on the side of his house since the front door was clearly not welcoming for mail delivery.

I know this was a part of his master plan. This was no accident.

If I fulfilled his exhibitionist fantasies, then good for me and for him.

I only remember that he had a huge hairy belly.

Rabid raccoon

As I placed the mail inside the screen door, a voice from behind demanded *"Don't move."* Great, I forgot my pepper spray today.

Do I accept my fate or make a ruckus so the homeowners could potentially save me?

A slow gaze back revealed a uniformed man holding a long pole with a lasso on the end. With deft precision, he lassoed a maniacal raccoon by my feet.

That thrashing raccoon hanging by its neck while it was carried to the truck still haunts me to this day.

I'll take a clown over a raccoon any day of the week.

Social Security day

They were like zombies.

I could see them in the rearview mirror and there were

lots of them.

Elderly folk demanding their Social Security checks before I could personally deliver them to their mailbox.

How did I know if they were who they said they were? Is it illegal to give people their mail out of order?

Typically I would drive away from the savages but every once in a while I would get caught off guard and out of fear, I would give them whatever they wanted.

A quick puke

A bad hangover and a lot of walking don't mix.

I had attended a Guns N' Roses and Metallica show the night before at Giants Stadium.

I drank my share of Jack Daniels. I thrashed to the insanity that was early '90s Metallica.

I put up a good fight for an hour but eventually I relented. I discovered a patch of woods, stealthily immersed myself in them, and took care of business very quietly.

I slickly covered the evidence with leaves and brush.

I bet nothing grows in that spot to this day.

Insane dog through the mail slot

It was kind of fun.

I would take the day's mail, loudly open the mail slot, and wait. Wait for the insane dog on the other side to emerge.

Once the mail was placed about a quarter of the way

inside the mail slot, Cujo would do the rest and pull it through. Then, I assume, he devoured it all and collapsed among the ShopRite and Kmart flyers and the PSEG bills.

One morning Cujo wasn't around.

And the garage door was open.

Game on.

It was inevitable. He was going to run out of that garage and take my leg off.

Sure enough, he slowly appeared and approached me like a pissed off jaguar.

I remembered what I was taught at mail carrier school. Turn your satchel towards your attacker and grab the pepper spray.

Satchel was turned but I couldn't locate the spray.

The dog jumped on me, I stood my ground and he went to town on the mail that peaked out of the top of the bag. I let it all go down, willing to go to jail for mail fraud as long as I lived to see another day.

The dog never attacked me.

But he ripped the shit out of that mail.

Turns out, he just hated mail.

Flooding an elderly women's toilet

This was really bad.

Like, if I owe one person in the world the most sincere apology, it is this woman.

Don't hate me based on what you are about to read.

From time to time I get really bad intestinal issues, like I'm going to go right here and now moments. It's a Van

Veen family trait that traces its origins back to a small town in Holland in the 1850s.

I've been much better the past few years. I think it's due to the fact that I eat much less white bread and pasta. Who knows? What my poor wife has witnessed over the years.

My shift was coming to an end that day and it hit, just like it always hits, out of nowhere and violent. There were no public restrooms within a short distance so desperation kicked in.

Desperation just makes it worse.

When I'm desperate I do stupid things.

Like knock on a random door and ask an elderly woman to use her bathroom.

She was clearly terrified.

I didn't have to wear a mailman's uniform so she had to trust that I worked for the post office.

I rushed into her bathroom, took care of business, flushed, and washed my hands.

The toilet wasn't fully flushing.

I finally grasped how dumb I was to have stopped here.

I panicked yet again, rushed out of the pink-tiled bathroom, and ran to my truck. I told myself I could avoid ever seeing her again by sneakily delivering her mail for the remainder of the summer.

She called my boss and he was waiting for me when I returned to the office an hour later. He asked me to confirm the story, assuming the lady was crazy.

I told him it was true.

He laughed uncontrollably. I just about cried out of

guilt.

I feel worse right now than I did even then.

> ***Chew on this:*** Life is all about experiences. Trying out new things can be rejuvenating. Seek them out whenever you possibly can.

GROW

CHAPTER 11

FALLING OFF THE LADDER

Our greatest glory is not in never falling, but in rising every time we fall.

—Confucius

October 12, 1997

Two weeks prior, my wife and I had just moved into our first home in Somerville, New Jersey. It was the ideal location on so many fronts.

Both of our families were within an hour's drive.

We'd be in the suburbs and have a sidewalk.

A Target, Costco, and Bed Bath & Beyond were within a 3.7-mile radius.

We both worked for large corporations with a convenient seven-minute commute to work for me and eleven minutes for my wife.

I don't remember us ever making an official decision to buy this home. Although that's how I have felt about all of the big decisions in my life. There is never a meeting with an official vote tallied or a, "Yes, let's do this" high five. It just kind of happens or wears you down to the point of "I guess so." There's little fanfare or pomp and circumstance.

Is that normal?

On a whim we had hooked up with a real estate agent who agreed to take us on a local house tour; we put no pressure on ourselves to find *the* home. I think our motivation stemmed from a parent's throwaway comment that went something like, *"You're just throwing your money away when renting. Why not buy a starter home and think of it as an investment?"*

We looked at one house that was clearly leaning, another that was on a hellish and busy thoroughfare, one that was haunted, and one that had a life-sized poster of Cher in the kitchen.

After each visit, the conversations between my wife and I were not too unlike an episode of HGTV's *House Hunters* where nothing is ever good enough for the spoiled and uninformed couple.

"He wants clean lines and will not go over their firm $150,000 budget."

"She wants character and at least three bathrooms."

"He has visions of a man cave, a three-car garage, and a billiards room."

"She wants a Craftsman with a Cape Cod feel but the function of a split level."

The only difference was we weren't forced to look at only *three* homes and weren't forced to have to choose one of those three homes. (That's a true *House Hunters* inside joke that I hope at least one of you gets.)

Along the way, I mastered the art of pretending to understand.

Yes, I love the concept of two-zone heating and forced

hot air.

I nodded my head in acknowledgment that, yes, that is in fact a load bearing wall.

Yes, it's great that this property includes a French drain.

There was no way I was going to admit to not knowing a thing, even if a sly follow-up Google search on my mobile had yet to exist.

At this point in time, I was 25 years old, a husband of one year, and 100 percent clueless when it came to home ownership responsibility. My father didn't have the "fix-it" or "grasp how things work" genes and he passed down those non-genes to me.

Fortunately my in-laws had more than enough handyman DNA to go around so I knew we had some support should we take the plunge. I had no idea how I would properly repay them for their services other than loving the hell out of their daughter. That would have to be enough.

Weeks after our inaugural home-buying tour and with nothing promising on the horizon, we came across a house on our own that was "For Sale by Owner." I didn't know much, but I knew that meant no realtor fees so we had an opportunity to save some cash. We called the owner and immediately had an appointment to see the house the very next day.

We toured the home, which had been owned by a recently deceased woman (to this day I don't want to know if she passed in the house or not), and even though it was old (1950s Cape Cod) and awfully appointed (a killer shag rug) we observed that it had "good bones" (let the record show that I said it out loud first) and clean lines (no billiards room). We agreed to purchase the home for $115,000 (sigh, the nostalgia of home buying in 1997).

A quick "How not to bargain" side note

I asked the seller to throw in a crappy push lawnmower I spotted in the shed while we were negotiating the price. He wouldn't budge, and I gave up on the spot, tail between the legs. I don't think I've attempted to bargain since.

Back to October 12, 1997

I know this was the exact date because I have a rather sick photographic memory that is grounded in all memorable sports moments. That day, I vividly remember watching the Pittsburgh Steelers play while standing on a ladder, glancing through the picture window at the front of our house.

Why was I watching TV on a ladder?

The curb appeal on our home was only decent at best, and it needed more. Gardening, or as I referred to it at the time, "landscaping" (it felt more masculine), didn't even enter into the equation. I was completely satisfied with the "green bushes" that lined the foundation and that I had already (cover your ears garden friends) sheared into gorgeous lollipops. Throw in 13 or so inches of mulch (high five, Dad) and we were on our way.

I still remember the heavenly scent of cut yew branches mixed with cedar mulch.

My wife and I eventually determined that adding shutters would up the curb appeal. If I remember correctly, they were given to us by my parents and who would turn down a free anything when you are house poor?

Once the decision was made to hang the stunning forest green shutters, I proactively and confidently volunteered to be the one to do it. I wasn't allowing my wife to get on that ladder and show me up and the in-laws would be needed for more difficult tasks at a later juncture.

Did I have any idea how to do it? Hell, no.

There was no YouTube as a guide.

This was a huge moment for me.

This was my first chance to show my new bride that she married a man who could "do it himself." I knew my wife quietly feared that she would be living a life of outsourcing simple tasks like light bulb replacement. Failure was not an option if I wanted my lady's respect.

So I grabbed my ladder, my new drill, a couple of screwdrivers, and the shutters and got ready to enter real man territory. As I climbed up that ladder and caught a glimpse of the football game through the front window, I remember trying to work out a plan where I could subcontract the work and then hit up the couch, beer in hand. It took all of my considerable strength to push on, but I did.

I'm not sure how, but I managed to get on two of the shutter sets without electrocuting myself and without putting a hole through my fingers. I just drilled random holes and don't remember using a level or tape measure.

I could have quit then and there and been content.

I then moved on to the side of the house near my driveway (this is a key piece of information as you'll see in a minute) and was all set for shutter set number three.

As I climbed the ladder for the third time, I glanced over a bunched up white t-shirt that was filling in the hole between the air conditioning unit and the side of the window (remember, we were house poor). I could see my wife sitting on the couch, and as she stared back at her handsome and resourceful husband, I gave her a cocky head nod as if to say, *"I got this shit."*

What I learned soon after that was that "having that shit" means you proceed to fall off said ladder with the fall perfectly framed through the window while your wife looks on in confusion and then horror.

Yes, I fell off that ladder.

Luckily and even more comically, I fell on top of my car, proceeding to roll off the car's hood and directly onto my neighbor's lawn. One shutter was broken in the melee but it was still in better condition than my already fragile ego.

What started as an exercise in confidence building ended in an exercise of brutal self-loathing.

After gathering myself and calmly getting to my feet, my wife popped outside to make sure I was okay. I laughed it off and gave the proverbial "no biggie" nod and pretended to get back to work.

Once my wife was safely inside the house, I allowed my meltdown to ensue. A contained meltdown from the outside but damn if I didn't give myself an internal tongue lashing.

"Could you suck more, John?"

"Your wife will never respect you, a-hole"

"If you can't do this John, what can you do?"

The shutters never made it onto the side of the house. I couldn't maneuver the ladder properly to be able to screw them in. I justified it by the fact that no one would ever notice from the streetside view and my wife never brought it up again.

Initial test failed.

I really started to worry that maybe an apartment was a better choice for us. That, or our money budgeted for groceries each week had to go toward a permanent handyman fund. And he/she would have to live in the tiny shed in the backyard for ease of access.

Panic had set in.

That following week, still mentally beaten down from Shuttergate, I set out for the local garden center to pick up some mums. I couldn't possibly screw up placing two baskets on the front porch, could I?

Once there, I innocently picked up a holly shrub on extreme clearance and casually read the label. It was kind of nice, green, and trimmable, and the label so eloquently indicated that it was easy to grow.

Do I need to worry about this "zone" deal?

Maybe I could add a few shrubs to the front bed and call myself a landscaper. I couldn't possibly do any serious damage with just a shovel. Would that make up for just a little of what I couldn't do inside the house? Do I pursue the outside as my domain since the risk is so small?

Two days later I was back at the nursery buying another holly.

The seeds of a gardener were planted.

Chew on this: Do not let the fear of failure get in your way when pursuing your passion. It's simple: when you fall off that ladder, get back up.

CHAPTER 12
THE HOME DEPOT BOOK

If one cannot enjoy reading a book over and over again, there is no use in reading it at all.

—Oscar Wilde

It's the spring of 1998.

The world is "Gettin' Jiggy Wit It." *Titanic* continues to dominate at the box office. Major League Baseball season is upon us. And my newfound interest in "landscaping" hasn't waned over the winter since the horrors of "Shuttergate."

Take note of the fact that I use the term "landscaping" rather than "gardening." That's exactly how I referred to my newfound interest in plants at that time.

Like so many uninformed people today, I associated the word "gardener" with an older woman snipping daisies while wearing a large-brimmed hat and kneepads.

That could never be me. I liked landscaping, which is like totally masculine. I liked cutting lawns, firing up a gas-powered trimmer, using a backpack leaf blower unnecessarily on my postage stamp-sized lawn, and maybe planting some "green bushes." There was no room for flowers. While I was pursuing an interest in "bushes," I was by no means heading down the road of gardener.

While still armed with that ogre-like mentality, I made

a trip to The Home Depot to pick up, um, something. While impatiently waiting in the never-ending checkout line, I spotted HD's *Landscaping 1-2-3*. I pretended to read it in order to pass the time while some dude argued with the cashier about the price of a pipe fitting.

As my turn to pay finally arrived, I didn't put the book back on the shelf as expected. Some powerful outside force made me place it on the checkout counter. It was an impulsive purchase that was decided for me, not by me.

I still truly believe that.

When I got home, I opened up my new book for some light reading while devouring my everything bagel and cream cheese. I recognized the bleeding heart shrub from my leaf report a decade earlier. When I saw the azaleas I was back in my grandparents' yard. All sorts of good memories flooded in.

I quickly learned the difference between evergreen and deciduous.

I quickly learned the difference between annual and perennial.

I quickly learned that those were yews in front of my house along the foundation and not "green bushes."

I started to drag the book with me wherever I went. I'd read a page here and a page there. It was the ideal bathroom read, the ideal book to leaf through while watching bad TV, and the ideal book to bring outdoors as the weather warmed up.

I never put it down.

This book was so killer. It even looked great with its green binding as it rested on our slowly developing bookshelf.

We may have been house poor, but that $14.99 investment was so worth it.

Eventually and fortunately, it became my gateway book into "real gardening books."

Around that same time, with the greatest of intentions, I had picked up another book, *Home Maintenance for Dummies*. Don't laugh. This wasn't a gag gift from my family. The internet hadn't truly blown up yet, so the *Dummies* series was as good as it got.

I managed to understand some of it (translation—the real basics) but certain diagrams made me throw the book down in frustration. Why was I so incapable of understanding basic plumbing or electricity? I realized then that I really was missing the spatial relations and common-sense genes.

I really was hopeless *inside* the house.

As a result, the *Dummies* book was thrown away.

I would seek refuge and take comfort in my precious landscaping book. I couldn't do too much damage while digging a hole and throwing a plant in it. Nothing could blow up or cause a fire. My family was safe from harm while I was outdoors.

After many hours studying and memorizing my Home Depot book, I actually started to map out a plan for my own yard. It mainly revolved around adding/replacing shrubs since my property at the time had sufficient mature trees. I had identified the shrubs I was interested in purchasing without a concern as to where they would be situated. Planning for conditions (soil, sun, and so forth) was not taken into account.

Just a minor detail was missed.

The very first nongreen-only shrub I acquired was a 'Nikko Blue' hydrangea. I was pulled in by its fantastic blue blooms and bright green foliage. This was a big step for me because for the first time, I openly embraced the idea of flowers. And I wasn't even wearing a large sunhat when I made the declaration. Maybe my grandfather's influence was bigger than I'd realized. Maybe I had to fall off of a ladder in order to discover it.

I followed the steps on how to plant a shrub, right out of my handy-dandy book. I dug a hole twice the width of the rootball. I dug a hole as deep as the rootball. I watered the hole before inserting the hydrangea. I stomped down on the watered hole to remove air pockets. I placed the shrub in the hole and evaluated how it looked from all angles. I placed the dug-out soil back in the hole and formed a moat around the perimeter of the now-filled hole for ease of watering.

I was money. I was a landscaper.

If my memory serves me correctly, the hydrangea blooms were pink when I purchased the plant, but I had plans to "make them blue" based on my newfound knowledge of soil pH gleaned from the HD book.

I felt like a magician. The yard was immediately transformed.

Who needs shutters when you have hydrangeas?

I even proceeded to replace my boring evergreens shrubs with scarlet barberry shrubs I had learned about in my wonderful HD book.

Something good was happening here.

> **Chew on this:** Do you find yourself intrigued by the birds in your backyard? Get a bird identification book from the library. Do you love grilling? Dive in and research different methods online. Have you quietly wondered if you could paint a landscape? Buy a canvas and some paints. Just start.

CHAPTER 13

MOVING ON FROM THE LAWN

Be the change that you wish to see in the world.
—Mahatma Gandhi

And The Home Depot fun continues.

Once you own a home there's an unwritten rule that one must visit a Home Depot at least once a week. Even if you're like me and struggle to replace a light bulb, you have to confidently walk into HD on a weekend morning, happily acknowledge the greeter, and hit up the aisles with your cart or orange bucket in hand. It's annoyingly burned into the male DNA to love these excursions and to get all giddy when perusing drill bits.

I freakin' hate Home Depot. Always have, always will. It reminds me of my shortcomings and the smell screams, *"You have a lot of projects to do and not the first clue where to begin."* It's intimidating, emasculating, and stressful and makes me want to go back to the good old days of renting an apartment.

But I found a way to manage the HD excursions. I would fool the other HD shoppers into believing I was willingly entering on my own accord. A confident gait works wonders. After entering the store and before the wave of anxiety could set in, I would simply make a quick hard right and head outside to the garden/landscaping department.

That was my domain. I had been cutting a lawn most of my life, and I even knew how to replace the string on a grass trimmer and operate a gas-powered leaf blower. I was comfortable in this environment. I'd hang there, revel in my comfortability and then once my confidence peaked, I could quickly get whatever else I needed in the store before the anxiety revealed itself.

During one particular Home Depot excursion, I became enamored with the Scott's 4-Step Program for the lawn. While I was just discovering the joy that is plants, my heart still belonged to the lawn.

I read through one of the Scott's brochures and within minutes I was convinced I needed to treat for grub control and crabgrass. You mean if I follow these simple instructions I can get a lawn as green as those on TV? Where do I sign up? And where was this when I was a kid?

Within a year, I had diligently followed the instructions and applied all four recommended "feedings" and my lawn kicked all sorts of ass, not too unlike the greens at Augusta.

I was the envy of the entire neighborhood. If you were to drive by my house on a late Saturday afternoon in the spring or summer, chances are you would have seen me sitting on the front stoop, beer in hand, ogling my lawn.

On top of the Scott's plan, I also began to regularly spray each individual weed with Roundup. You mean to tell me there is a weed killer that kills the weeds but doesn't kill the lawn? Holy shit. USA! USA! USA!

During year two of "Chemicals changed my life for the better," I woke up one morning and to my horror, saw a perfectly straight line of yellowing dead lawn smack dab in the middle of the front yard. It was clearly from one pass with the fertilizer spreader. It looked awful. I felt awful. This was supposed to be easy; just follow the rules and the grass stays green for life.

At that same time, we welcomed our first dog to the family. She was a yellow Labrador Retriever named Casey.

After we brought her home and took her outside for her inaugural pee, I felt a wave of uneasiness. As she set up for urination #1, she started to sniff and chew on the grass.

Up until that point, I was in denial that I was placing a foreign substance, of unknown origin, onto my grass four times a year in rather large quantities. I couldn't let this puppy, who relied on us for survival, get anywhere near the stuff.

Just like that, an immaculately green lawn lost its luster.

It didn't require too much reading and research after that to see that chemicals were not the answer. I felt ashamed to have been so naïve to what I was putting into my lawn. I felt like a cliché, the suburban man overly consumed with a green lawn. As if that green lawn somehow defined me as a man.

And yes, I also blame Scott's. They made me do it with their manipulative marketing campaign. They knew I was vulnerable and they took advantage of that.

If I had to identify a turning point or the key moment when my passion for gardening kicked into overdrive, this would be it. I was at the cusp of fully embracing plants and looking to create an actual garden. At the same time, I was losing interest in maintaining the perfect lawn.

I put away the chemicals for good.

We eventually moved into our current home a few years later. It is 2-plus acres of property with a monstrous lawn to contend with. My obsession with plants continued to grow and evolve but that imposing lawn still had to be addressed.

I wanted to maintain a lawn so my children had a large place to play but I had no interest in putting forth a chemical effort, smarting from my days as a Scott's disciple.

I decided to seed in year one (it was a patchy mess) and then take it from there after witnessing the results.

By the following spring, the grass had filled in enough to make it a true full-blown "yard." Was it perfect? Not at all, but it was so overwhelmingly large that I didn't bother trying to come up with a plan of attack.

Actually, that's not true. I followed the age-old adages that have stood the test of time:

- Cut the grass at its highest setting.
- Leave the grass clippings on the lawn and let nature take its course.
- Enjoy the fact that the clover, a "weed," provides green cover, a source of nitrogen, and a flower source for the bees.
- Acknowledge that the dandelions are "flowers" and

should be honored rather than branded as evil.

Because the lawn was so large, watering by hand wasn't even an option. Neither was the ridiculous cost of installing a sprinkler system. I could live with some brown in summer.

My lawn has never looked better. I literally do nothing other than cut it once a week in spring/summer/fall.

That's it.

It works.

All of the time saved is dedicated to the garden and plants where I have a chance to wave my wand and make beautiful art.

> ***Chew on this:*** Are you trying new things? Are you scratching that itch? It can open and provide opportunities, and invite new people into your life.

CHAPTER 14

SPIDERS

Spiders so large they appear to be wearing the pelts of small mammals.

— **Dave Barry**

I wasn't the kid who was intrigued by or ever sought out any type of critter. I didn't play in the dirt and I didn't pick up worms. I had friends who would turn over rocks in the woods just to see what creatures could be found underneath. When they did that, I squirmed, looked away, and thought about baseball.

In fact, there is quite a legendary story in Markowski family lore about my deep fear of butterflies as a young lad. My mother reminds me of it regularly, now that she sees that I enjoy nothing more than chasing the Monarch butterflies around in my own garden. As a kid I refused to step outside if there were any signs of a butterfly nearby. If I was forced to confront my fears by my unsympathetic parents, I would physically shake and fall down in a heap.

Side note: Lepidopterophobia is the fear of butterflies. If it has an official name I couldn't have been that crazy. Nicole Kidman allegedly suffers from this fear. It's not so weird anymore, is it?

I remember one giant spider that resided on a jalousie on our enclosed porch. It was there for weeks and we all completely avoided the porch, other than making sure the spider hadn't left its perch. I couldn't sleep at night. I had nightmares. I vowed to avoid the outdoors for eternity.

I don't know how the spider issue ultimately resolved itself, but I do know that I'm not alone in recalling just how traumatized we all were by that mammoth arachnid.

Our region had awful caterpillar problems when I was young. The black, furry critters would completely cover our trees in spring/summer and it was a regular occurrence to see them smashed all over the roadways. They were creepy and everywhere, and they infiltrated our lives from every angle.

One day we kids were forced to stay home from school making sure all windows and doors were shut so a helicopter could fly overhead and spray some toxic chemicals on all of the town's trees. One neighbor protested by sitting on her roof. I thought she was nuts then but I really like her now.

I broke my right wrist in first grade sliding down the giant playground slide. My body went down the slide as the kids pushed me, but my arm stayed behind, hooked around the top of the slide. I remember Patty Huff greeting a crying me at the bottom of the slide and escorting me to the nurse's office that afternoon.

This was the same Patty Huff who was mercilessly

mocked throughout middle school and all the way through high school. I friended her on Facebook years ago and was happy to see she was doing okay. Sadly she passed away soon after that from a medical issue I never fully understood. I wish I had thanked her for her kindness back in 1979 and, that I had stood up for her more in school.

These words ring hollow now because I did nothing. I don't get to pat myself on the back now.

When I broke my wrist, I had an overwhelmingly strange skin reaction underneath my cast. I was convinced it was the result of a stray caterpillar that had found its way up my arm. I would laugh until I cried, fall down, and beg my mom to make it stop. She sympathized through tears of laughter. The day I got that cast cut off was the most freeing day of my life.

When I found gardening or when it found me, I quickly realized I had to confront my fear of the critters that inhabited the soil. Worms were fine, and I learned early on to appreciate their worth. I would pick them up, pat their squishy backs, and place them back down so they could do their good work to improve my soil.

The spiders were another story. I squealed a lot at first. I would throw my trowel at them and run away. There were a lot of false alarms as my paranoia grew.

Then one day I spotted a mother spider scurrying with baby eggs still attached after I nearly decapitated her with my shovel. This changed everything. I had immediate sympathy and felt her fear. I was a lot bigger than she. So what if she has eight fuzzy legs and always looks pissed off. She's just trying to survive.

So we reached an unwritten agreement. I left them alone if they promised to announce themselves quietly: no jump scares, no surprises.

This arrangement worked beautifully. We were able to coexist. I came to sympathize with their purpose in life. They ate all of the bad bugs even if I didn't know what those "bad bugs" were. I came to appreciate that they had work to do just like I had work to do.

I lost all fear of spiders.

This newfound comfort with spiders allowed me to play hero to my wife soon after.

It was the day after Christmas in 2002. My newborn son was 5 months old and my wife was still on maternity leave. It was our first Christmas as a "family."

I was at work and my wife was home with our son, watching him roll around and coo under the Christmas tree. This Christmas tree was a beauty. It was the perfect shade of blue/green and flawlessly shaped. Its only drawback was that the needles were so sharp, we had to place the ornaments on the tree while wearing gloves.

The sacrifices we make.

We had cut the tree down weeks earlier on an official family outing. We have fantastic photos of triumphant me holding the tree in one hand and a saw in the other. A great shot of my father-in-law holding baby Jack in the snow. A borderline obnoxiously perfect holiday moment. But damn, how happy I am now that we took those photos.

Here's a tip for you all if you want to cut down your own Christmas tree. Sharp needles are a great means for protecting whatever wants to reside within the bowels of the tree. And more often than I realized then, spiders like to live in said trees. Like a lot of spiders.

The call to my office was straight out of a horror movie. My wife was whispering like she was holed up in a closet, trying to escape her captors. She and my son had taken shelter in our bedroom. It was the only safe place in the house. As she recounted, it started with a peripheral glance at something jumping from ornament to ornament and ended with the realization that there was a full-blown spider invasion. I can only assume all of the spider eggs hatched at the same time and they then agreed to set out and wreak havoc.

I jumped off my conference call and raced home. Fortunately for my family, I was less than ten minutes away.

I raced up the stairs, ignored the grisly scene in the family room, and consoled my wife. With the utmost confidence, I told her, *"I got this"* and proceeded to head back down the stairs and directly into the line of fire. I did so with a smirk on my face because this guy no longer had a fear of spiders.

I got rid of every last one of them.

I took off every individual ornament, inspecting each not only for spiders but spider eggs, and I carefully packed the ornaments away. I carried the didn't-know-what-hit-it tree out to the street, daggers from the branches and all.

I continued to monitor the house for weeks to ensure no stragglers were left behind.

My wife swooned when it was all done.

I was totally her Prince Charming.

We could go back to hanging-with-the-infant bliss.

Since that day, I have become the spider whisperer. Out here in the country, we get terrifyingly large spiders in our garage and in our basement, and they are good at stealthily sneaking through our front door.

All the family needs to say is "Dad" and I'm there with a paper towel. I don't kill them. I lure them into my paper-toweled hand, gently ball it up, and place them in their natural environment. They don't scare me no matter how hairy or sinister they look.

I'm currently considering going into the spider removal business. Who needs help?

> **Chew on this:** Do you explore what scares you? Lean into those fears and see where it takes you.

CHAPTER 15

COMMITTING A CRIME

The criminal is the creative artist; the detective only the critic.

—G.K. Chesterton

Prior to the crime I'm about to admit to in this story, I had stolen exactly two items in my lifetime. I'll assume the statute of limitations has passed for both since each crime was committed in the early '80s.

I'm now ready to confess my sins. I may ask my daughter to pass these along to the priest at church next time she hits up confession. She's Catholic and I'm not. Long and boring story, for another time.

And to my wife, kids, and all other family members, I apologize for dropping this on you in this way since you weren't aware of my criminal background. I'm prepared for the fallout. But you get why I did it this way, right? Story ideas trump human feelings.

If memory serves me correctly, both of these thefts occurred in 1983 when I was 11 years old. I blame my descent into a world of crime partially on peer pressure; all of my friends at the time were years older than I. I had to prove myself if I wanted to keep up with them. A suburban gang initiation if you will.

I also partially blame my parents for Crime #1.

The chase for grape soda

Growing up, soda was never to be found in our refrigerator. It was marketed by my parents as "bad for us" and loaded with sugar, which, of course, made me want it even more. Yet there were giant containers of Pathmark iced tea mix in the cabinets, which seems counterintuitive to the "no sugar movement."

I craved grape soda like you wouldn't believe. It's all I ever wanted to drink. If I was fortunate to be offered it at a birthday party or through a covert transaction in the woods at the end of Oak Avenue, I jumped on that shit without hesitation. It was like crack with the added benefit of a killer purple mustache.

So what would you do if you knew that your best friend had grape soda in his refrigerator and knew that the family was at the Jersey Shore for the week and knew where they hid a key to the easily accessed and hidden-from-view back door?

Of course, you would.

I did.

I recruited an accomplice (let's call him Glenn O) whom I subsequently pulled into the fire when I confessed to our breaking and entering a week later during a moment of weakness. I caved out of guilt. I hid from Glenn O for weeks to avoid getting my ass kicked. We're now friends on Facebook and the topic has never been broached.

The pursuit of Mike Jorgensen

The scene for Crime #2 was Kay-Bee Toys at the Paramus Park Mall in Paramus, New Jersey. It was our go-to for birthday gifts for friends and family of all ages. It's where I connected the dots on the Santa Claus charade when a certain handheld football game carefully tucked in the bottom of a see-through bag miraculously made it under our Christmas tree.

On this day, I had no plans to commit a misdemeanor when I wandered towards the baseball card display at the very front of the store. My mom walked the aisles with my sisters and allowed me to go off on my own.

As you already know, I was an obsessive card collector and I was very close to completing the 1983 Topps set through purchasing packs that spring and summer. I had a handwritten checklist of the cards I still needed to acquire, and I had it in my pocket at all times.

Mets catcher Mike Jorgensen was on that list.

As I leafed through a few random loose cards for sale for 10 cents, I saw him.

Seconds later he was carefully hidden in the sleeve of my long-sleeved shirt.

I don't know why I didn't ask my mom for ten cents.

While I felt guilty, I also felt proud of my bold and illegal move.

I hadn't told a soul until right now.

As I write this, it's the last week of the year where I will make my beloved "day-job-lunchtime-trek" to my local nursery.

One last opportunity to score a deal on heavily discounted perennials.

One last opportunity to take a selfie with an ornamental grass.

One last opportunity to dream up plant combinations.

One last opportunity to run from my "real" job and pretend I'm a garden designer.

One last opportunity to record an Instagram story happily revealing my purchases as they sit in the back seat of my Honda Accord and soil the backseat, resulting in complaints from my kids, whom I in turn ignore.

These lunchtime visits to the garden center go back over two decades and hold a warm place in my heart.

It's where I first learned the difference between a conifer and an evergreen.

It's where I first fell in love with foliage and learned to look beyond the flowers.

It's where my finely pressed khakis would get covered in mud that would result in stares from coworkers who questioned what I was doing during my lunch hour.

I can't even begin to name all of the plants I've discovered over the years through these trips, but each one of them offered an incredible sense of discovery and was, at the time, a vital piece to my garden design puzzle.

As I think back to the early days of lunchtime plant shopping, one of my fondest memories is stealing the plant tags of those plants I considered for future purchase.

Yes, another criminal enterprise. This makes three in my lifetime. That's a good ratio.

It was a simple process:

- Bend down to look like I am inspecting the plant and/or checking out the price
- Stealthily pull the tag out of the container with my left hand
- At that same time, run the right hand over the leaves of the victimized plant as a means of distraction
- Quickly remove the excess soil on the tag by squeezing the thumb and pointer finger and dragging them along the tag
- Drop the semi-clean tag into the pants pocket at the same time I stand up

Once I had a healthy collection of tags for the day, I would head right for the exit with my head down so this rugged mug couldn't be identified. I would head out making sure I wasn't being tailed by any vehicles. Once safely home or back to my office, I headed right to a computer so research could commence.

Why didn't I simply write down the names while at the nursery? I don't know. The tags felt like puzzle pieces that I could easily move around. They were easy reminders of what each plant looked like.

And stealing was hella fun.

After my research was completed, I would compile a list of plants to be bought the next trip. I left the tags at home and stored them in a plastic bag to be enjoyed at a later date.

Through the years, I have had a variety of different

getaway vehicles and all of them were on the small side. They got me from point A to point B. That's all I needed. A car was a necessity and not a luxury. I don't want to spend a lot of money on something that means so little to me. That money could go to another viburnum instead.

I am 6 foot 4 (*"and full of muscle"*…know that song?) and look funny in small cars. I can steer a car with my knees like no one else.

Imagine big me driving a tiny little car surrounded by recently purchased shrubs that are climbing out of each of the windows. It's a sight to behold. I can only imagine what people are thinking as I pull into the parking lot at work. It looks like a tiny jungle on wheels with the faint sight of an actual driver.

I have to be careful when allowing my precious plants to rest in my car for hours until the end of the work day. I have killed my share in the past due to extreme heat and for that, I am not proud.

To combat the threat of death and because my cars are not exactly the envy of thieves, I leave the windows down the remainder of the day in the parking lot so the plants can breathe. Even if rain is in the forecast, I leave the windows completely opened so the plants can grab a drink. A healthy plant is more important than the suffering that comes with a wet and smelly car.

When I am walking the grounds at my local garden center, I stick out like a sore thumb in my businessware; it's not the typical dress code when shopping for plants. I'd kill to be in my ratty shorts and t-shirt but workday lunch is one of the only times I am free to spend an hour or so just walking aimlessly through a maze of plants.

Sweaty pits be damned.

It's all worth it.

True story: A nursery I used to frequent fell on hard times financially. I don't know all of the details but the government had to intervene and shut them down. They must have been selling illegal hostas or something. Actually, I think I would shut them down for selling hostas at all.

Eventually the nursery reopened so I made it a point to check things out during another lunch break. As I approached the entrance, one of the owners asked me, *"Are you Brian?"* I laughed and said "Not this guy" and went on my way.

Weird.

Upon further review, I determined that they mistook me for a government inspector since I wasn't exactly dressed like a dude who was looking for the latest *Heuchera*.

On at least two more occasions, I was greeted in the same manner but instead of laughing it off each time, I gave them a slight nod and simply proceeded inside. I figured it would be fun to keep them on their toes and act like I was on official business. I'm not sure what they thought when I eventually rolled up with a cart full of bee balm, but I do know that I had fun.

I've had my fun and some shady times (wink) at the local nurseries over the years during my lunch hour. More than anything else, I valued the escape. The escape from the trappings of the corporate world and that mindset and into a relaxed environment that also happened to smell damn good.

> ***Chew on this:*** What is your means of escape? It can be a yoga class or trout fishing. Give yourself permission to make room for these activities no matter how busy your schedule may be. Fill that happiness cup.

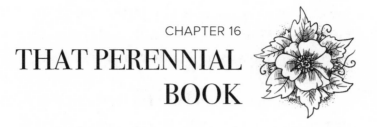

CHAPTER 16

THAT PERENNIAL BOOK

"Gardens are not made by singing 'Oh, how beautiful!' and sitting in the shade."

—Rudyard Kipling

If you were to put a newly sharpened spade to my head and force me to pick *the* one moment that transformed me from more-than-casual gardener to every-day-obsessive-gardener, it would be this:

A winter day in 2001 when I received *The Well-Tended Perennial Garden* by Tracy DiSabato-Aust in the mail from that cute little boutique bookseller, Amazon.

This was before kids entered the picture, when my wife and I could play footsie and read under blankets for hours on end without a care in the world. My book reading had evolved from mindless John Grisham and James Patterson novels to all gardening books, all the time. The Home Depot book was pushed aside as I started to spread my little gardening wings.

I was a sponge and notes were written on anything and everything in sight: birth certificates, cable bills, and mini notebooks adorned with strange pharmaceutical company labels.

Once *TWTPG* (my pet name) entered the picture,

my outlook on gardening completely transformed. That book spurred my obsession with perennials. That book forced me to toss aside all other interests.

I was all in.

For those of you who aren't familiar with Tracy's book, here is the summary pulled directly from Amazon:

Novice and experienced gardeners alike will benefit from Tracy's thorough details on the essential practices of perennial care—included deadheading, pinching, and thinning—along with growing information for new species and cultivars, on-trend garden design advice, a monthly planting and maintenance schedule, and details on native plants and gardening for wildlife. The Well-Tended Perennial Garden is a must-have ally in the quest for a beautiful, well-maintained garden.

I need whoever wrote that summary to write one for this book. That is spot-freakin'-on.

Up until that point, my idea of plant care was plant it, keep it watered, and pray that it stays alive. What is this deadheading you speak of, Tracy? And how the hell do I differentiate between that and pinching and thinning, Ms. Aust?

Many readers and wannabe gardeners may have been intimidated by all of this required work and maintenance, but I was immediately enamored. You mean I get to spend more time with my plants and I can tinker with them in a beneficial way? When and where do I start?

At the time I got my hands on this book, I had a

very small suburban garden with only a few random perennials. There was no rhyme or reason to what I planted or where I placed them in the garden.

But I was super psyched to learn that a few of these perennials were included in her book.

Geeky gardener warning: If you aren't a gardener, the following may bore you to tears. You may skip it. Or if you're open to it, you'll see an example of a man knee deep in his passion and maybe it will inspire you just a bit. It's your call.

The first plant I located was *Coreopsis grandiflora* and the first sentence blew my mind:

Tickseed (common name for Coreopsis*) needs daily deadheading.*

"Hell, yes" I remember declaring to no one in particular. That meant I got to come home from work each summer evening, wipe the corporate filth off of my body, grab my pruners, and do something with meaning.

I deadheaded (removing the dying individual flowers, which encourages new ones to grow) the heck out of those three plants. They looked perfect, without a sign of even one faded bloom. I never tired of the task and even began sneaking home from work at lunch to deadhead while I wolfed down an impossibly scorching Hot Pocket.

Another perennial I had mindlessly purchased and haphazardly planted was *Tradescantia* (common name spiderwort) because I was taken by all of the pretty purple blooms in the nursery. They looked okay once in my garden, but I became frustrated as the flowers seemed to curl up and disappear without reason.

Enter *TWTPG* and I quickly learned that the individual flowers on *Tradescantia* only last for a half-day and then the petals disappear.

Why did the plant label not tell me this? Do I need to stand near these plants at the nursery and warn potential customers? This was an outrage. It kicked off my distrust of garden centers and online catalogs and made me question their marketing ploys, which indirectly lead to my first book, *Perennials Through the Seasons*.

Feel free to go to Amazon now and check it out and maybe even consider buying it.

And yes, we'll talk about that book more in a subsequent chapter.

Once we moved to our current home, *TWTPG* became my bible and Tracy Disabato-Aust became my lord and savior.

She taught me the concept of cutting back perennials (cutting them down as they start to grow so they ultimately end up shorter in size and therefore are less likely to fall over when in flower). I did this with Joe Pye weed, false aster, sneezeweed, sedum, and others.

I even started my own series on my eventual garden blog entitled "Prune in June." June is the month for cutting back and I experimented with various pruning options, eventually sharing and comparing the results. I felt it to be my duty to share all that I learned from

TWTPG with the rest of the world, or at least the few hundred who read my blog regularly.

To this day, perennials dominate my garden.

I enjoy watching them mature from little babies to fully established plants. I enjoy taking those established plants and dividing them into little babies that will then mature into an established plant. The process continues for eternity.

I enjoy watching my perennials die. I love the blooms but I also enjoy the seedheads post-bloom. I love watching the birds devour the coneflower seeds in winter.

I love perennial experimentation in terms of design and individual maintenance. I move them around often seeking the perfect vignette. I prune them to the ground at times and will leave them untouched at other times.

Perennial gardening is who I am.

It started with the Home Depot book and reached obsession level with *TWTPG*.

> **Chew on this:** Go all in.

CHAPTER 17

BATHROOM READING

Always go to the bathroom when you have a chance.

*—**King George V***

Warning: the majority of the following story takes place in a public restroom. If you find that offensive, please feel free to skip this and move on to the next chapter. Just know you'll be missing out on a crucial part of my development.

I had it down to a science:

- First print a legitimate, work-oriented page.
- Then print the real "reading material."
- Walk to the shared printer carefully surveying nearby coworkers.
- Once at the office printer, first pick up the "work" printout.
- If there were no curious eyes watching me, also take reading material with the work printout prominently displayed on top of the stack.
- If anyone else was near the printer, just grab the work printout and leave the reading material behind as if it weren't mine. A follow-up trip could be attempted minutes later.

- Sit down with the stack and toss the work printout.
- The reading material could then be folded twice and shoved into the right front pocket.
- Walk towards the bathroom with the right hand lingering in front of the stuffed pocket so the bulge of papers could be hidden from view.
- Enter the bathroom, enter the stall, and pull the material from the pocket.
- Sit down and become educated.

It may be difficult for some of you to remember, but there was a time when we couldn't simply read from our smartphones when taking care of business.

If you wanted to read while using the facilities, it required some innovation and some stealth activities. That was what I was doing at work in the early to mid-aughts. I was reading the "Garden Web Forums" to learn as much as I possibly could about perennials, or fertilization, or the best means to protect a container plant through winter.

My move was to pick two to three discussions and print all of the pages that corresponded with those questions. I knew how to identify the go-to commenters. I knew which members would often quarrel over something like the definition of a conifer. I would become educated and be entertained all within the same forum topic.

If my folded papers had any real killer info, I would keep those in a special folder hidden in my cubicle. All other pages would be discretely discarded in the bathroom garbage can when I was done.

This period of gardening education may be where I learned the most. This was deeper than reading a book. This was a collection of real gardeners sharing real stories about their real gardens. It wasn't all pretty all the time. It was a lot about failing and the need to experiment in the garden.

For a fledgling gardener like myself, this was heaven. My family and friends were not gardeners. I had no one to share seeds or to talk garden design with. These forums introduced me to virtual friends who knew all of the Latin names of plants. Friends who would remember that I dealt with poorly draining soil and would recommend a shrub that could work for me. This was the beauty of the internet prior to the onslaught of social media.

I remember initiating a topic around the best ornamental grass for a beginner. I wanted nothing more than a name so I could then go out and purchase it without having to think too much.

I didn't get that. I remember being inundated with, *"What zone?"* and *"For what soil type?"* and "*Warm-season or cool-season?*" Not one person provided a simple answer. I quickly learned that wasn't the proper etiquette. I also learned that it's never that easy when it comes to a garden.

But what really invigorated me was that this didn't turn me off to gardening. It made me want to learn. I didn't really want the simple answer. I wanted it to be difficult because that made it that much more rewarding and enjoyable.

These forums also introduced me to gardening debate,

heated garden debate. The "Roundup supporters" versus the "I hate Roundup contingent." The only-native-plants people versus the I'll-grow-whatever-I-want crew. These discussions were a fascinating read and opened up my eyes to the fact that it was more than, *"Should I, like, plant a* Sedum *in my front yard or whatever?"*

All of these discussions informed me as a gardener. They made me want to take photos of my garden and share my results with others. They made me want to have a say and to document my own journey as gardener.

I loved crafting a forum post where I could ask a question and inform readers at the same time.

I loved the consistency of writing on the forum every day.

I loved the interaction with people who shared a common interest.

This was the precursor to my future blog.

This was the precursor to the "Obsessive Neurotic Gardener."

Chew on this: Are you a part of a community where others share your same interests? Participate in a way where you feel comfortable, even if you lean toward introversion like me.

CHAPTER 18

A BLANK SLATE

*I try and reduce myself to an almost blank slate
and hope to God that I am creative.*

—Ben Kingsley

All I knew was the suburban lot.

I grew up on one in northern New Jersey and all of my friends and family grew up the same.

Soon after getting married my wife and I moved to the suburban town of Somerville, New Jersey.

It was all suburbia, all the time.

Just enough lawn to justify the purchase of a gas-powered lawnmower.

Sidewalks and aboveground pools.

Short and narrow driveways.

Nosy neighbors and yard upkeep competitions.

As you know by now, assuming you've read this book in chronological order, the Somerville home is where I designed my first garden. It's where I tinkered and where I made all of the mistakes a newbie gardener is expected to make.

Looking back now, it was easy to create that garden. The garden beds were already there when we moved in. The soil was great and easy to pierce with just a shovel. While available plant space was limited, it made it less daunting as I ascended into the early stages of a gardening obsession.

Just as I had that garden to the point where it was "done" (yes, I know now that a garden is never "done") my wife and I made the executive decision to get out of suburbia. Between overnight stays in quaint hotels and numerous day trips, we fell in love with rural New Jersey, specifically Hunterdon County. It had charm for days, large lots, fewer strip malls, and a slower pace to life.

At the time we made this decision my son was two years old and we knew that we wanted to have a second child. Our current home, even after adding an addition (that's fun to say), wasn't going to fit us all comfortably. Not only did we need more living space indoors, we needed more outdoor space so the kids could run wild and breathe some good ol' country air.

It was time to make that move.

I was so excited to tackle the creation of a garden on a large lot. I was excited to have unlimited possibilities. My status as "gardener" was going to be put to the test and I was more than ready to take it on.

We ended up purchasing a home in mid-construction. It didn't have a plant in sight, other than a few scraggly trees in the front yard. This was a blank slate to end all blank slates.

The idea of a blank slate extended beyond the garden.

We didn't make the move alone. We had hatched a plan to have my father-in-law, my brother-in-law, and my grandmother-in-law move in with us temporarily. All had fallen on hard times financially (not of their own doing, long story), and this was a chance to allow them all to regroup and get back on their feet. As stressful as the coordination would be, we knew it was the right thing.

Add a pregnant wife soon after the move to the equation and you had a recipe for some chaos.

But we all ultimately survived one another, and I'm proud to say that the plan worked beautifully. We found a way to make it through with two young children and a full house. Everyone got back on their feet and thrived just as we had hoped.

Family first worked.

That ended up being the easier task to tend.

I had no idea where to start in the garden.

I wanted to get back to suburbia and get back to smaller. But it was beyond too late because, you know, all of those documents and stuff were signed.

Upon moving into the house and in a move that defies logic, the first plant I added was a camellia along the foundation. Not only had I never considered a camellia before, I missed the fine print indicating it would only survive to zone 7. We were zone 6B. I must have forgotten that we lived in New Jersey and not in Georgia.

That camellia died within weeks.

The following spring arrived and I was ready, I thought, to finally attend to operation "Blank Slate." The only problem was, I still had no idea where to begin. There was no logical starting point. I knew I needed to build the bones of the garden but my bones knowledge was limited. At a minimum, I needed anchor plants but I had no idea where to anchor them.

Because of this, I made a controversial decision. I decided not to start a garden that year. The thought terrified me as I feared losing all of my knowledge by not actively gardening for a year. What if I lost my mojo by not exercising my gardening muscle for so long?

Instead of focusing on the plants, I focused on the hardscape and adding a few large trees for privacy. We had a new front walkway installed, much wider and curvier and more interesting. We built a large deck on the back of the house. These installments naturally created garden beds and that is where my country garden journey would begin.

Spring arrived the following year and I was finally ready to get planting. I had garden beds prepared and I'd sketched out ideas. I'd taken my first trip to the nursery with the goal of focusing solely on shrubs. They would be the backbone of the garden. Trees would have to come later, after we hit the lottery.

I arrived home with a car full of shrubs, giddy with anticipation. It had been too long. I missed the dirt, the callouses, and the filthy fingernails.

I did that thing that gardeners love so much: I arranged and rearranged and rearranged again all of the shrubs, still in containers, until it looked just right. I wanted it to look natural but orderly. I did my best to anticipate what each shrub would look like at full size and to take that into account when siting them. It's a fun but maddening task when piecing together a new section of garden.

And then I dug the first hole. Scratch that, I "attempted" to dig the first hole. The shovel went into the dirt and—nothing. A few specks of dirt was all that was removed. The soil was all shale, clay, and impenetrable objects that must have been covertly buried by the builders.

I immediately wanted my down payment on the house refunded. How was I ever going to plant a garden under these conditions? More importantly, what would survive in these conditions? Knowing I had tons of space to fill, I felt like throwing in the trowel at that moment.

Fast forward a few months and I discovered the solution: a six-foot shale bar with a terrifyingly sharp point. That and a dash (or ten) of hard labor allowed me to get some plants in the ground. I beat myself to death, but I got it done. I also questioned whether or not I could sustain this new "process" and build a full-blown garden.

Fast forward another year and 75 percent of what I'd planted the year before didn't survive the winter. My initial assumption was that the very cold winter destroyed these weak-excuse-for-plants. So I bought more shrubs and replaced the so-called weaker ones with so-called stronger shrubs.

That failure didn't bother me as I ventured into the

creation of new garden beds, farther away from the house and from the deck. I quickly filled them with more plants.

I did everything fast and without care for cost. I needed a real garden, and I needed it fast.

Fast forward another year and real panic ensued. I couldn't ignore what was happening. Plants continued to die at a rapid pace.

Deer found their way to my property and took advantage of my deer-friendly plantings.

I couldn't mentally, physically, or financially keep up this pace. I needed a new strategy.

After countless hours online and conversations with informed nursery workers, I learned that poor winter drainage is the leading cause of killing plants, more than cold temperatures.

That meant that I shouldn't force plants to embrace my conditions. A garden's conditions should dictate the plant choices and not the other way around.

As simple as this seems now, back then it was a wake-up call for uninformed me. Everything worked in my first garden at the old house. We had no deer and had great soil.

Here in the country, the soil didn't drain at all and the deer and rabbits were everywhere. I had to embrace that, and I soon learned that my plant choices weren't as limited as I thought.

One category of plants in particular would thrive here.

One category of plants would naturally fit in here.

One category of plants would bring my garden to new

heights.

They are known as ornamental grasses.

They saved my life.

Chew on this: Get those hands dirty. Don't waste too much time planning and perfecting your approach. Just do.

CHAPTER 19

THE OG

Ambition is the path to success, persistence is the vehicle you arrive in.

—William Eardley IV

I like to think that ornamental grasses saved my life.

They kept me off the streets and in the garden. I can only imagine where I'd be today if those ornamental grass hadn't kept me happily engaged with my shovel.

The grasses revealed themselves at a time when I needed them most and for that I'm eternally grateful.

After struggling mightily to find plants that could thrive in my garden conditions (poor-draining soil, mostly full sun, and ravaged by deer and rabbits) I took to the 'net in search of help. The standards or most common plants available at the local nurseries weren't cutting it. I had to dig deeper, pun fully intended.

Geeky Gardener warning #2: Brace yourself.

As a side note, this search was conducted at a time before I discovered the wonder that is the native plant sale. That would have made my life a lot easier. But we'll discuss that joyous discovery in a chapter soon to follow.

There was, and still is, no better escapism than winter plant shopping. As those delicious catalogs appear in the mail in December and January (or if I simply head online to the company's website), I like to curl up with a large mug of hot cocoa (extra marshmallows), put on a classic holiday movie, throw on my favorite wool sweater, sit crisscross-applesauce in front of a raging fire, and gleefully circle (or add to the cart) all of the plants on my wish list.

I'm just kidding; it isn't like that. I would never add extra marshmallows. That would be weird.

Back in the early days, I automatically skipped the "ornamental grass" section and headed right to "shrubs" and "perennials." In my yet-to-know mind, the grasses were for more formal gardens or for weird collectors. They would never work in my garden.

Could I have been more wrong? The answer is a definitive "nope."

During one winter, I was holding one of my cozy plant-shopping sessions and had filled my virtual cart to the upper end of my pre-assigned budget. As I surveyed the cart and played around with the number of plants to be ordered for each (ensuring only odd numbers were ordered), I did one last run through the "Sale" section and saw that there were red grasses for sale at a dramatically reduced price.

Red grasses? Color me interested. I only thought of grasses as green.

The full name of this grass was *Panicum* 'Rotstrahlbusch'. Could there be a more intimidating name? Was that done on purpose to keep us amateur gardeners away? Could I, in my right mind, purchase a plant that I couldn't pronounce?

After some cursory research I learned that "Rots" (as

the cool kids call it, I've since learned) "turned" red in autumn and wasn't a true red grass. But that was okay; my interest was piqued. I tossed three in my cart and placed my order.

Fast forward to spring and my plants had arrived. The grasses were tiny little green plugs and without giving it much thought, I just planted them in the garden. Better to get them in the ground than have them sit around waiting for me to figure out a logical location for them.

As I'm wont to do, I forgot about them until August when, out of the blue, those tiny plugs, now 18 inches in height, transformed into a killer red hue that immediately grabbed me. I naively never thought of grasses providing fall color in the garden, and this was my first taste of how wrong I was.

The big test, however, would be the following spring. Would these young and immature grasses survive the wet and cold winter? So many others before them had failed, and I was conditioned to expect the worst.

They did come back, but it took until late April for them to show signs of life. I had left them for dead but did my best to remain patient and wait it out.

What I learned that spring was that grasses are grouped as either "warm-season" or "cool-season." *Panicum* species fall under the warm-season category so they don't emerge until the soil temperature warms up in midspring.

Those grasses went absolutely bananas in year two. By that July, they were at least four feet in height. They developed red hues even earlier than the year before.

They flowered in late summer at a time when flowers were seriously lacking in my garden.

I was taken by their texture and how they played with other plants. They were the perfect backdrop to summer-blooming perennials. They were the perfect foil, foliage wise, to large-leaved shrubs.

And the movement of grasses—I didn't see that coming. Even the slightest of winds would result in a grass dance that brought my garden to life. I didn't know the power that was movement in the garden until I saw just how much the grasses energized it.

I'm getting all sorts of giddy just thinking back on that time of discovery.

On more than one occasion, I watched the deer approach the grasses with the intention of making them lunch. As they closed their eyes and opened their stupid deer mouths, they were quickly rebuffed and deeply offended by the sharpness of the grass blades. I could see them shudder and curse.

The deer despised the ornamental grasses.

And I had a new favorite plant.

The love affair just exploded from there.

I remember being late to an REM concert (wow! life comes full circle thinking back to my forced listening of this band back in high school) because I was so consumed by planting all of my newly purchased *Miscanthus* 'Morning Light' in the dead of summer. I nearly passed out after the concert that night from exhaustion and it wasn't from excessive dancing or passionately singing "Man on the Moon."

If you search long enough on my blog, "The Obsessive Neurotic Gardener," you will find a parody of "Baby, It's Cold Outside" written about, you guessed it, an ornamental grass.

In fact, if you read through my blog you will quickly learn that my garden is centered around my passion for ornamental grasses.

No plant looks better in death than ornamental grasses. Their ability to hold up in winter and absorb the ice and snow with a subsequent display that is bordering on dreamlike is what gets this obsessive and neurotic gardener through the winter.

My next book will be about ornamental grasses.

It will most likely be called *Ornamental Grasses Saved My Life*.

Because they really did.

> **Chew on this:** Stay persistent. Keep that fire burning inside at all times. Don't let anything or anyone stop you.

CHAPTER 20

MISSING WALLET

Do ya' feel lucky, punk?

—Clint Eastwood

Here is the story about my lapse in judgment that resolved itself through supernatural intervention. Realizing this was a gift from above, I made life changes that day which I've carried with me ever since.

"Hi John, it's Uncle George. I have your wallet, give me a call when you get this message?"

What
The
Hell
?

I never intended to listen to any messages on our home phone. I was in the process of calling the first credit card company to cancel their card since my wallet had inexplicably disappeared during our ride home from vacationing in Connecticut. I played the message to get it out of the way.

"How is this even remotely possible?"

While I had an enormous sense of relief, I was convinced that someone had created this long, elaborate, and complex riddle, and it was up to me to solve it before calling him back and getting the answer.

Why was someone putting me through this?

So I tried my best to piece it all together, but I had nothing.

I'm sorry; let me back up a bit.

Years ago, while on our way home from a stay in Chester, Connecticut, I pulled the family-mobile off the road and into a local gas station to refuel for the four-hour trek home. And even though I grew up proudly not pumping my own gas (Jersey baby) I kind of cherished the opportunity to pump while out of state. I felt manly and in control. God knows I have to jump on those opportunities when they present themselves.

Three minutes later our trip home commenced.

If my memory serves me correctly, we listened to the New York Mets game on the radio and probably played the license plate game. I also yelled at my son four times to stop kneeing his sister because no, she isn't purposely trying to annoy him.

Two and a half hours later after the joys of driving on Rt. 95 through Connecticut and New York, we pulled into a Starbucks in Oakland, New Jersey.

A need for coffee beckoned us.

And the kids probably had to pee. They always have to pee.

The truth is, and I realize this now, fate pulled us into that parking lot.

Thank you, fate.

If I'm a decent enough writer and if I've successfully employed the art of foreshadowing, you've figured out what happened next.

No f'n wallet.

I was convinced it fell through that black hole between the driver's seat and the driver's door so I frantically searched there, for twenty-three minutes too long.

My wife had to verbally slap me in order for me to grasp the reality of the situation.

The wallet was gone.

The only plausible explanation was that it fell to the ground back in Connecticut after I paid at the pump (f'n self-service). No chance I'd see that again.

Wasn't that vacation fantastic, family?

While in deep mourning over the loss of my wallet, we quickly and silently walked into Starbucks, ordered what was going to be sad-tasting coffee, and allowed the kids to drain their bladders.

This ride home was not going to be fun.

We considered canceling all of my credit cards on the ride home in fear that someone was already living high on the hog up and down the Eastern Seaboard with my Visa. But I think I convinced myself that the wallet had to be somewhere inside the car and I'd be able to find it once we pulled into our driveway. So we put off the phone calls.

After we arrived back home and I came to the realization that this was not going to end well, meaning no wallet was found in the car, I grabbed the phone to start the highly enjoyable process of cancelling credit cards. As I picked up the phone to call the first credit card company, I noticed we had a voicemail. I contemplated skipping it and coming back to it later but instinctively hit "Play" as a means to temporarily put off the inevitable.

So now we are caught up.

I'll let you read the exact voicemail message one last time.

"Hi, John, it's Uncle George. I have your wallet, give me a call when you get this message?"

Care to try and piece together how this all played out, Encyclopedia Brown?

No, Bugs Meany had nothing to do with it.

Truth is, you would never be able to figure this out on your own. So with one last spoiler alert warning, here is how it all played out:

My wallet did not drop to the ground at that gas station in Connecticut. I left it on top of the car after having placed it there while I was pumping the gas. I, of course, have zero recollection of doing this.

The wallet managed to stay on top of the car from that gas station in Connecticut all the way to New Jersey. A two-hour car ride on Rt. 95 in stop-and-go traffic.

Chew on that.

It fell off when we pulled off the highway and were on our way into the Starbucks parking lot.

An off-duty police officer saw it while driving at an intersection and scooped it up as he was driving in one fell swoop.

The previously mentioned Uncle George (who, by the way, I call "Uncle" but he is of no relation. Do you do that?) was a retired police officer and his graciously provided PBA card was inside the wallet.

The police officer who picked it up happened to be best friends with my uncle's son (a not-really cousin), also a fellow cop.

He gave the wallet to my not-really cousin and asked my not-really uncle to call me.

My uncle stepped out from the wedding he was attending to take the call. After receiving the message from his son, he called me and left the life-changing message previously referenced. He then returned to the wedding, sat back down at his assigned table, and continued his conversation…with my parents.

Holy divine intervention, Batman.

This was clearly my last warning to get my shit together. These kinds of things don't just happen. I'm sure there is some scientific reason how to the leather adhered to the metal roof due to the heat of the sun and blah blah blah, but I ain't buying it.

We've driven past the exit for that Starbucks dozens of times and had never stopped once. If we hadn't stopped, that wallet might still be on Rt. 287 in New Jersey with the cash long spent by some hitchhiker or vagabond.

Ever since that day, there have been three life changes I immediately implemented and still actively follow today.

I refuse to wear shorts without pockets. That only leads placing important objects in strange locales, such as a roof.

I haven't placed a single item on top of any vehicle. Just a week before that we'd lost an entire bag of freshly picked apples because of the car roof issue. Not to mention the hundreds of coffees I've lost. Or my laptop.

Most significantly and out of dire necessity, I created an OCD-like ritual to ensure that I have all of my essentials on my person at all times.

The ritual requires me to say out loud:

"Keys, wallet, phone, ID."

I then tap each pocket to ensure they are all securely in their appropriate locale. The wallet and ID (for work purposes) are in the front left pocket. The phone is in the right front pocket. The keys are in the back right pocket. And the back left pocket is reserved for receipts, change, and so on.

There is no deviation from this arrangement.

I must do this upwards of 100 times a day and I haven't lost any items since implementing this ritual. If you ever see me mumbling quietly to myself, just know not to interrupt. It's similar to how you should never interfere with someone who is sleepwalking.

But know that I'm okay.

The concept of ritual chanting has been extended to other aspects of my life as well.

"Alarm on, garage closed, refrigerator door shut, lights off, dog has water."

The more it rhymes and is sing-song, the better.

"Call exterminator, text Mom, return library books, pay Tom."

And because a lot of my world revolves around gardening, I've used this technique there as well. Here is a sample reminder of what to do/not-do in the winter garden:

"Continue watering, avoid compaction, shake the snow off brittle branches."

Yes, it sounds a bit bizarre but holy hell, is it ever effective. It completely removes the stress and anxiety for those of us who have a knack for misplacing our belongings or forgetting simple tasks very easily.

And my garden is better for it.

Chew on this: I have no point here, really. It's just a fun story to share. It kills at cocktail parties. But I can say that ritualistic chanting has become a great life hack.

LOVE

CHAPTER 21

SNEAKING PEONIES

*I like gardening—it's a place where I find myself
when I need to lose myself.*

—Alice Sebold

My family was one of ten families staying in a large multitiered home directly on the beach in Virginia Beach, Virginia. It was a reunion for my wife's side of the family. There was a good mix of infants, tweens, teens, and adults. It was chaotic and fun. There were some dramatic moments and some conflict, but that's the price of admission when you allow this many people to reside under one roof at one time.

I'll refrain from any specifics in fear of my in-laws being offended. Just know, for purposes of this story, that it was wacky and odd and, at times, super tense.

Someone may have disappeared during a rainstorm. Someone may have had a run-in with an airline and their no-fly list. There were a few awkwardly silent dinners with many retreating to the comforts of their tiny bedrooms to avoid further conflict.

My favorite moment of hilarity was a severely clogged toilet that required a visit from a local plumber. When he arrived, my wife was mixing a giant vat of baked beans as she informed him of our issue. Yes, I'm immature but c'mon, imagine what he was thinking at that point.

"Beans, beans they're good for your heart, the more you eat the more you…"

I found survival through drinking. I took to making pineapple and vodka for myself, my wife, and my brother-in-law without ever asking if they wanted it.

Cheers to family dynamics!

My family, fortunately, was able to stay out of the drama. We're Switzerland. That's kind of our thing and we've been recognized as such throughout the years. We enjoy relationships with each and every family member regardless of what inter- and intra-family conflict is hot at that moment.

The reunion was held over the course of a week. I had to head home early due to work obligations so I only stayed for four days. My wife had to be a single parent for the other three days, tending to our four-year-old son and not yet one-year-old daughter. I know what you're thinking, poor me, missing out on all the fun.

The idea of being alone in our home for three days without children was intoxicating. I could eat whatever I wanted, whenever I wanted. I didn't have to change diapers or shuttle the children to daycare. I could go to the bathroom with the door open. I could own the TV without the need ever to put on the Disney Channel. I could shower in peace and sleep in peace.

My nights would be my own after work and the freedom was going to be borderline overwhelming.

Did I eat Taco Bell and drink beer for three nights straight?

Did I watch all of those movies my wife has no interest in ever watching?

Did I go out with the boys?

Did I have the boys over and burp together while watching the big game?

No, I didn't.

I did something much more exciting, much more manly, and dare I say, scandalous:

I came home from work that first night and changed into my comfortable shorts and favorite t-shirt.

I made sure my social calendar was clear. I made sure I didn't owe anyone a return text or phone call.

I quietly sneaked out to my car and laid tarp down on the back seat.

I made sure I had enough cash so there wouldn't be any record of any transaction.

I drove 15 minutes to my destination, barely breathing out of anticipation.

I stepped out of my car and scanned the immediate area. There wasn't one car in sight. I'm clearly here alone, and that was great news.

I walked in through the gorgeously adorned gate.

It was time to do some plant shopping where I could finally buy those peonies I've had my eye on for some time.

I planted them under the cover of night. I took photos of them on my flip phone for future sharing.

I didn't tell my wife a thing. She can't know that I'm having that much fun. She also can't know that her sneaky husband buys plants behind her back.

Because that's, like, really weird.

Listen, I was never a "hang with the boys" kind of a guy in the first place, but this was taking it to an extreme. I spent the entire three days buying plants, planting plants, and strategizing about plants. I told no one that I was home alone. I wanted no contact with the outside world.

And the photos of the peonies I referenced were the first photos I had ever taken and ultimately shared with an audience. This was more than a hobby. It was becoming a passion, a passion that flowed through my veins 24/7.

When you are sneakily gardening, you know you've arrived.

Postscript: My wife struggled mightily with my daughter sleeping at night the remainder of the reunion/vacation. She eventually lost her mind, and I developed enormous guilt. I don't think to this day that my wife has any memory of my gardening exploits while she was single parenting. That's good.

I flew from Newark Airport in New Jersey to Norfolk, Virginia, the last day of the reunion and met up with my family at the airport. Once we were back together, the four of us immediately drove eight hours back home to New Jersey.

Yes, I dreamed up that plan and took care of the logistics.

Yes, I want credit for that killer idea.

I drove the entire way home so my wife could finally relax.

I don't think the kids said a word the entire car ride.

I am a great husband and father.

> **Chew on this:** Whatever you find yourself doing during "me" time, pursue that fully. Find more ways to incorporate it into your life. Spend less time on the nonsense.

140

CHAPTER 22

THE THINGS WE DO

Though you can love what you do not master,
you cannot master what you do not love.

—Mokokoma Mokhonoana

When we have a true passion for something, we go to great and often bizarre lengths to feed that passion. Actors remain in character off camera. Baseball players take swings in the batting cage *after* a game. Directors insist on the forty-seventh take of a throwaway scene. Salespeople practice their pitches in front of a mirror.

Dudes buy peonies on the sly and hide it from their wives.

Contrary to popular belief, we obsessive gardeners are insane. We just hide it well and stay under the radar. Our significant others, more than likely, have no idea the means we'll go to in order to tend to our plants. The stereotype of the Zen gardener is horseshit. We're all kinds of crazy and willing to do whatever it takes to feed our need for the dirt. We're also wickedly resourceful.

We will garden through lightning storms.

We will draw up plans while sitting on the toilet.

We listen to music to pump us up to…dig (or is that just me?).

As I look back over the past two decades and recall

141

some of my stranger exploits, there are a few that really stand out. Actions that, on the surface, are stupid and even at times dangerous. But that's what we do when we're in the zone, when we're doing what we love, when we're answering our calling.

Frozen peas

I don't think I'm oversharing by telling you that I had a vasectomy. We're tight like that now. Once my wife and I had our son and then our daughter, we accepted our blessings and cut bait, literally. I had no qualms taking care of business and scheduled my appointment for three months after my daughter was born.

The appointment fell in March, smack dab in the middle of "March Madness," the annual college basketball tournament. I envisioned three days of sitting on the couch, taking it easy, while watching basketball all day and night. Fortunately my son was young enough at the time that I could easily lie to him about the purpose of the surgery.

At the same time we mapped out the snipping of my *vas deferens*, we also scheduled the installation of new hardscape and trees for our newly purchased home. It was to be a new bluestone walkway, new beds surrounding the front and back of the home (yes, I could have done it but they were already going to be there), and a bunch of pine trees along our property line that would provide privacy and a solid windbreak.

With the laws of karma fully in place, my surgery and

the start of the landscape work were scheduled for the same day.

I got snipped early in the morning (awake the entire time, go me). I chatted about March Madness with the urologist as a strong smell of smoke was in the air.

And because I'm tougher than most, I drove myself home afterwards.

When I pulled in the driveway, no one was home and I was dreaming of nothing more than couch, basketball, and pizza.

But the landscaping crew arrived minutes after I settled in on the couch. They knocked on the door so we could walk through the plan. I was in some pain in my nether region but I pushed on. Knowing it was important that I kept all of my stuff properly iced, I grabbed a frozen bag of peas and stuffed it down my Champion sweat pants and ventured outside. My memory is that I successfully hid the sound of the shifting peas as I walked, but I could be wrong.

Suddenly basketball meant nothing. The vision of new garden was coming to fruition right in front of my eyes. And the peas couldn't have been more soothing.

I ended up outside with the crew for hours. I lied to my wife when she asked if I had been resting.

I took a notebook outside the next day. I sketched planting plans. I continued to wear my peas.

Gardening > Basketball

Stitches

Every spring I take one day off in June and dedicate it solely to my garden to-do list. There's nothing else on the planner beyond that. I've been known to call it "Christmas in June." Even if it rains on this special day, I still spend the entirety of it outdoors. It is my way of honoring the Markowski Mulch from my childhood.

On this June day, my wife would be at work and the kids would be in daycare, which conveniently happened to be located on the campus where she worked. They would leave at 7:30 a.m. and return by 5:30 p.m.

So my gardening timeline ran from 7:31 a.m. through 5:29 p.m.

I had big plans. This would be a day of enjoyable hard labor.

One of the tasks was to create a new garden bed on the side of the house. That area was filled with large rocks and compacted soil. I had my shale bar, shovel, and a pair of indestructible gloves.

I beat the heck out of that soil, in a good way.

I cleared large stones and planned to use them decoratively throughout the garden.

Then one of those rocks split in half as I carried it. It cut me good on my wrist. I watched blood spurt out and did my best to remain vertical.

I ran into the house and got a towel.

I clearly needed stitches.

Remember, no one was home.

I needed to drive myself to the hospital. There was no other option.

It was only 9:45 a.m.

My day was ruined. The one day *only for me* all year.

I drove to the hospital but I didn't tell my wife until I got there so she wouldn't worry. I ate three granola bars during the drive. I thought I needed plenty of fuel since I had lost so much blood.

The intake nurse didn't believe my story. I guess a cut on the wrist is a red flag. I had to retell the story at least five times before it was accepted as truth.

I eventually received seven stitches and was home by 3:30 p.m.

Without hesitation, I got the shale bar, the shovel, and one glove. I dug holes and planted with one arm. It was awesome. It was enlightening. This silly hobby, pastime, and passion was much more than that.

I needed it, bloody arm and all.

Paradise by the dashboard lights

Time is everything.

Any free time is ideally allotted to gardening. Even if it is five minutes, those five minutes add up and one can get a lot done that way.

I had planted five bee balm plants one afternoon in a spot that I thought was perfect. They would receive full sun, plenty of moisture, and would have room to grow as they spread through their underground rhizomes (look it up, nonplant people.)

Mission accomplished in less than 15 minutes.

I then took a shower. I think a lot about plants while

in the shower (um). While reviewing my just planted bee balm, I convinced myself that I did it all wrong. I had to move them to make the voices in my head go away. But I had no free time available for the next few days. My anxiety grew by the minute. This had to be squelched.

Even after getting all nice and clean in a gloriously warm shower, I headed back outside.

It was pitch black and cold.

I got in my car and threw on the headlights and maneuvered the car just right.

My newly planted bee balm were on full display, even at 9 p.m. The light from the car framed them beautifully.

I dug them all out.

I got back in the car and maneuvered it just right again.

An open section of the garden was under the spotlight.

I replanted the bee balm, this time in the correct spot.

I parked the car.

I showered again.

I drank a beer.

I slept like a baby.

Chew on this: Do you research recipes during downtime on a conference call? Is there a common theme of the podcasts you listen to in the car? Do you pull to the shoulder on the road just so you can take a photo of a tree and put it on Instagram? Take note.

CHAPTER 23

GOING NATIVE

The more that you read, the more things you will know. The more that you learn, the more places you'll go.

—Dr. Seuss

I started out gardening like your prototypical spring gardener we all see at The Home Depot on a Saturday morning in April. I'd buy a bunch of pretty plants, stick them in the ground in some bloody awful symmetrical pattern, fertilize them to death, and then be done with it.

I AM GARDENER. (For a day, at least.)

I slowly evolved from that gardener to one who was buying books and checking them out of the library on a weekly basis. I then elevated my gardening game to a whole new level by pruning and pinching perennials daily and experimenting with different combos that I would obsessively rearrange. Soon after I was stealing plant labels from nurseries and bringing them home to further my plant knowledge.

Truth be told, my plant palette was still limited. The only plants in my purview were those that I could find at my local nursery or that I easily recognized when shopping online.

But the more time I spent in my country garden and visiting local gardens, the better feel I developed for my new digs; specifically, how said digs fit into the larger landscape of my town, county, and state.

That observation led to the recognition and general understanding of the "native plant." The best definition I can find for a native plant is this (from garden writer Andy Wasowski):

Native plants should be defined as those that have evolved and adapted to a specific location and have remained genetically unaltered by humans.

My simple definition is this: a plant that naturally grows where you live.

Once I understood the native plant, all of those signs around town advertising "Native Plant Sale" made a lot more sense. It was a no-brainer to check one out.

It's Mother's Day and the plan is to make mom breakfast in bed and then head out for the day so she could also enjoy some peace and quiet. The kids are five and two, so you get it. That weekend also happened to be the opening of the native plant sale at Bowman's Hill in Bucks County, Pennsylvania.

My plan: We'll go out to breakfast, hit up the plant sale, and then hit the playground before heading back home. Everyone would be happy.

In preparation for the trip, I studied what was available for purchase at the plant sale. For my garden, I knew the plants had to be deer resistant, had to prefer full sun, and had to tolerate a wet soil. I compiled my tentative list and had it in the back pocket of my shorts (no more pocketless shorts for this guy, thanks lost wallet caper).

The kids had no intention of enjoying themselves at the sale. They made that clear immediately.

Why are we buying plants here?

I'm too full from breakfast; I can't walk.

This is boring.

We had to park a far distance from the sale on a narrow road with heavy traffic. Our car was hanging precariously off of the side of the road, dangerously close to falling into the abyss below.

There was an endless parade of plant shoppers with massive carts pulling their purchases down the road. I knew there was a high probability one of us was going to be hit by a car or knocked down a cliff. I corralled the kids and used my best parenting move to keep them safe: fear imbued with the worst-case scenario.

None of the other shoppers had children in tow. I should have recognized then that we needed to get there earlier and that bringing the kids was a colossal mistake. But we pushed on.

Upon arriving at the plant sale, I recognized that the plants were presented in alphabetical order. Supplies had severely dwindled. I made it a point to talk to no one for fear of having to pronounce the plant names out loud, knowing I'd butcher them all. I kept my head down and tried to hide my list under my sleeve.

My son, to his credit, created a killer tune entitled *"This Is Boring"* and he proceeded to sing it for all shoppers to enjoy while they plant shopped.

I was ready to bolt or heave the kids into the nearby woods until I was done. I settled on "Grab and Go" and quickly threw a bunch of *Amsonia* plants into my box without giving it a second thought. I think I also nabbed some *Asclepias* before heading towards the cashier.

I'll spare you the details of the remainder of that shopping trip but the kids have never accompanied me to a nursery or any other plant sale since that day. Daddy does that on his own now.

We did go the playground and after some fatherly scolding, all was forgotten.

The *Amsonia* kicked ass almost immediately.

That perennial is my favorite to this day. I have an ever-expanding collection and won't be stopping anytime soon.

I had no idea at the time, but that day changed everything for me when it comes to plant selection. Not only had I discovered a killer plant in the *Amsonia* (Google it right now for full effect) but I had my gateway drug into native plants.

I went on to read all I could about the benefit of native plants and have added so many more to my garden over the years. They lend a natural look to the garden. They require significantly less maintenance in their native habitat. They draw in more critters than the nonnative plants.

As happy as I was to have discovered my new favorite plant and as happy as I was to discover a new pool of plants from which to choose, it felt even better to have evolved.

It started with a move to a more rural setting.

I observed and dove into my new surroundings with vigor.

I did a little research, and I asked some questions.

I grabbed a random plant and the stars aligned.

I even have a funny memory attached to the discovery.

That's all you can ask for in life.

Chew on this: Do me a favor right now. Go into your Google search history and look for patterns. What do you spend hours researching and reading about? What do you spend hours doing? Do more of this.

CHAPTER 24

THE SPREADSHEET

Basically, our goal is to organize the world's information and to make it universally accessible and useful.

—Larry Page

I've worked in corporate America for 20-plus years and I'm not its biggest fan. The rigidity, the routine, and the phoniness and the backstabbing take their toll over time. There are times when I want to burn my khakis and my sensible shirt in order to eradicate the stench of insincerity.

On the other hand, it provides a steady paycheck. It has allowed me to build up my 401(k). I have a great healthcare plan.

Still, it's a daily internal battle to accept that this is who I am. I never wanted to be here in the first place, yet how can I complain when I've never missed a recital or a game and my weekends are almost always job free? I understand how fortunate I am, yet I don't want that to make me stay there much longer.

Escaping the grind is where gardening comes in. When I'm in the dirt, I'm only in the dirt. I'm incapable of negative thought. I'm free and I'm my best me. I don't have to provide a weekly status update and I don't have to join another mindless conference call. I don't have to build a project plan and there are no deadlines.

Just endless opportunities with zero judgment and zero performance reviews.

But I've learned that you can take the boy out of the finely pressed khakis, but you can't take the finely pressed khakis out of the boy.

I've been managing my plant collection, or garden if you will, through a carefully curated Excel spreadsheet. I keep it updated regularly. I reference it before I set foot outside each and every day.

I've been asked to share the template on numerous occasions and I refuse every time. This corporate-like inventory is sacred to me and while I resent the fact that I have to leverage my holistic skillset (yes, that was an intentionally corporate phrase), this gardener can't survive without it.

At last count, I have 171 different plants in my garden. The numbers fluctuate dramatically in spring and fall as I add newly purchased plants and account for those I've killed. My go-to move is to add a new plant to the spreadsheet the day I purchase it with a plan to update it fully within that week. It must always remain in alphabetical order by botanical name. If there is a matching botanical name, the alphabetization then extends to the cultivar name.

Nerd, I know.

OCD, I know.

You're bored with this story, I know.

But here's the thing: the consistent updating and research of this spreadsheet actually allows me to memorize plant facts that I can recall on a moment's notice. Logging all of my garden exploits has aided in greater retention of information, not unlike taking notes in middle school.

Ilex verticillata *'Berry Poppins' requires* Ilex verticillata *'Mr. Poppins' (quite the stud) in order to produce those highly desired berries.*

Before you ask, I've already read your mind.

How do I remember which winterberry is which out in the garden?

Why, I reference the "Location" column in my spreadsheet and for 'Mr. Poppins', it states *"under playroom window."*

John, do you think I can grow Miscanthus *'Variegatus' in a partially shaded location?*

Friend, I have data and metrics that back up the assertion that it will flop if placed in too much shade.

My Boltonia asteroides *regularly flops by the time it blooms in August. What can I do to prevent it?*

Through multiple tests, I've been able to discern that cutting it back aggressively in June (almost to the ground) results in significantly less flopping. Thank you, Tracy Disabato-Aust.

When fall arrives, I sort the "Winter Care" column and only address those plants that actually require winter care. All the others can confidently remain untouched until spring.

When spring arrives, I can access the "Pruning" column and remind myself which shrubs can be pruned "after blooming only" and which can be "cut back in spring" without fear of removing future flowers.

I have a "Division" column, which helps me keep track of when I divided perennials or when I'll need to divide other perennials.

But what really makes this spreadsheet magical is the history I'm able to retain.

I know that my *Lobelia siphilitica* displayed its first blooms in mid-August in 2010 but bloomed three weeks earlier in 2011. I love knowing that for some odd reason.

I know that my crabapple tree, on average, only blooms for 10 days each year. And I know that it bloomed from April 13 to April 23 back in 2012.

I know that I attempted to move a butterfly weed plant in 2010 only to see that it got the "X" a year later, meaning it didn't survive. If only I had read the "Misc" cell, which frowned upon even trying to transplant this perennial.

I know that I didn't cut down my coneflowers in fall and allowed them to remain up all winter starting in 2011, the year I embraced winter interest for the first time.

How cool will this information be in 2051, assuming Microsoft Excel still exists that far into the future?

I know the effort to create and maintain this spreadsheet has been worth it based solely on that look a visitor gets when they set foot in my backyard and see my garden.

They are blown away 100 percent of the time.

It wouldn't have been possible without my freaky need to be organized.

> *Chew on this:* I've been heavily mocked by other gardeners for this unnecessary bit of organization. I don't care, it allows me to enjoy it more. I'm just being me. Are you okay with just being you?

CHAPTER 25

FINDING TIME

A man who dares to waste one hour of time has not discovered the value of life.

—Charles Darwin

It's very rare that I'm blessed with large chunks of time to tend to my garden. Life gets in the way.

There's that thing called the day job. Society tells me I need to attend basketball games and teachers' conferences. The dog requires a walk every now and then. The family wants face time as do the friends.

Because of these requirements, I need to schedule my gardening time and I need to do so in small chunks. That's where I get the best ROI.

The scenarios look like this:

I've got a half-hour before heading to work in the morning.

I have fifteen minutes between conference calls.

I have seven minutes before the family emerges outside and insists that we depart for our vacation.

Those tiny pockets of time are crucial in terms of prioritizing what needs to get done. The most pressing tasks need to be accounted for first. Those priorities can also change because the garden never sits still. It is a living and breathing entity that consistently keeps me on my toes.

To account for this scheduling and prioritization, I set a schedule each week where I identify my potential "gardening available time," or GAT as it's known in my household.

Each GAT is assigned between one to four must-do tasks depending on their anticipated duration of time.

Of course each task time length has been measured and analyzed over the years.

Of course it is all logged in Excel.

You know me so well already.

A typical GAT might look like this:

10:00 Prune the viburnum
10:12 Deadhead the salvia
10:21 Weed around the front steps

Or it might look like this:

1:35 Plant the grasses
1:50 Water the tomatoes
1:57 Add the petunia to the container on the deck
2:03 Come to grips with the Japanese beetle infestation

Oftentimes I'll mix garden tasks with other life tasks when it makes sense to do so.

It can look like this:

3:34 Leave to pick up daughter from school

3:41 Research water needs for a clethra shrub

3:45 Leave school with daughter safely secured in vehicle

3:56 Relocate clethra shrub based on research findings

Once I know the appropriate tasks have been scheduled, I no longer have to worry about them. Even if something else comes up and I can't attend to them during their assigned time slot, I can easily move them to another GAT with a few mouse clicks.

By now you've picked up on the fact that I'm a stickler for organization in the garden. Yes, it goes against all that I've said about the garden being a true escape. When we escape we typically don't want to work too hard or be consumed with keeping track of items on a spreadsheet. But the organization is what allows me to relax.

If I've got everything logged, from the plants in my garden to the tasks that need to be tackled within a week's time, I simply have to reference my list and do what it says. The guessing work is removed, and I can just shoot down the spreadsheet and do what I need to do.

Have I mentioned I like organization yet?

Chew on this: There is always time. It's never an excuse. You know this so remove it from your tool box of excuses. If you wish to adopt some form of GAT in your life, send me an email and I'll set up a consultation.

CHAPTER 26
AN OPEN LETTER TO MY BROTHER-IN-LAW

It ain't no fun if the homies can't have none.
—Snoop Dogg

Here's an open letter I wrote to my brother-in-law years ago. We still laugh about it today. Also know that he recently purchased ten ornamental grasses to surround his pool based on my recommendation. He used a coupon code I shared with him since I am such a frequent shopper of the grasses.

Just happy to spread the love.

Dear "Brother-in-law" (name removed to protect privacy and curious onlookers),

I hope you realize what you have stepped into. Things will be dramatically different from here on out. Life as you know it, or knew it, is gone. And it all changed the moment you sent me this text (verbatim):

"Thanks for the *Panicum* tip. Thoughts on either Karl Foerster or fountain grass?"

Sigh.

I've been waiting for this day for a long ass time.

You are no longer just my BIL, you are part of something

much bigger now. A secret society of sorts, one in which we duck out during family functions and all I have to say to you is "Rots" (more on that later) and we both know exactly what we are talking about. The first rule of Grass Club is that you don't talk about Grass Club. Grass is no longer what you cut once a week in spring and summer. It goes much, much deeper.

The fact that you live a stone's throw from my humble country abode makes a lot of sense now. Fate brought you here. For too long it was just me and my silly named grasses. Now I have a neighbor who gets it.

Remember that movie *What About Bob?* I'll be a kinder and safer version of that lunatic. Just don't be surprised if I'm peeking in your window looking for a chance to talk about cool-season vs. warm-season grasses.

In fact, I've already taken the liberty of sharing my massive grass collection with you. You don't know it yet, but one of the *Panicum* 'Rotstrahlbusch' I had set aside two years ago with the optimism that I could give it to someone in the future...

...is now in your possession.

You are most welcome. And by the way, it is known among us grassophiles as "Rots." Wait until you see what she looks like in all her glory in July.

You know, you remind me of a young me. Just dipping your toes into the world of plants but with a desire for information and an interest to know more than the common folk. And since you've been saving me from myself by acting as our handyman for the better part of two decades now (and your four-year-old son helped me lay tile last week), consider what I'm about to tell you as small payback for your generosity.

Here are five things that will happen to you over the next six months. It will be confusing and exhilarating at the same time but just allow it to wash over you.

1. Odd numbers. While secretly planting your grass I noticed two *Salvia* planted nearby. Soon you will learn the mistake of your ways and make it three. And you will look at everything in the world in terms of odds and evens and realize odds always feel better.

2. You may like the look of mulch now but soon you will see your young plants fill in and want to add as many more as possible. You'll also soon realize more plants equal fewer weeds and *that* is the only real solution to combating the weeds.

3. You will realize flowers are fleeting and that there will be a need to focus more on foliage. I will smile like a proud parent when you ask me about bugbane.

4. Our conditions suck, like big time. You will fail with many plants and I will let you do it. It is part of the learning process and a vital step to becoming a true gardener. It will eventually lead you down the path to native plants. I predict within a few years you will have at least one *Amsonia* in your garden (or sooner if the plant fairy pays a visit one night).

5. This one will excite and frustrate. Like me, you have a large property here in the New Jersey countryside. There is always room for another garden bed. Dreams of sweeping curves and borders will dance in your head. Embrace it. It stimulates the mind and leads to killer

forearms.

I hope this letter finds you well and I hope you truly are a convert. It is magical, and I've got a ton of plants with your name on it.

P.S. I hope you're cool with me sharing your garden in the future with millions of readers all over the world.

> ***Chew on this:*** Sharing your thing with others doubles your enjoyment. There is nothing wrong with being a mentor and a mentee at the same time.

CHAPTER 27

THE LEMON

If life hands you lemons, make lemonade! Words to live by, especially when you kept in mind that the only way to make them into lemonade was to squeeze the hell out of them.

—Stephen King

Old family photos are a sham. We always look so happy and thrilled to pose for the pic because golly gee, everything is super great. We must capture it properly so it can't ever be forgotten.

Over the ensuing years, we embellish the heartwarming story in our minds by attaching memories to said photos that we all know are sketchy at best.

"I love this photo. Oh my god, that trip was so much fun. Those apples were like the best I've ever had, even with all of the bees flying around our heads. Remember how funny and silly it was when Dad almost fell off of the tractor? What an amazing memory."

Except it wasn't fun or funny.

The apples were sparse and absurdly overrated.

Both of you kids freaked out over the bees the entire time even though we all know they play a huge part in producing the apples in the first place.

Dad was livid when son pushed daughter and almost knocked her off of the moving tractor. That is why Dad almost fell. No one laughed at the time and we all stopped talking to one another for a good two hours.

Oh, that's not how you remember it? Enough of this revisionist family history you hypocrites.

If I had to estimate, the inauthentic photo backstory is true like 87 percent of the time. I do my best to bite my tongue as we all pore over old photos or videos, not wanting to kill the family's memories. Who am I to ruin it for everyone else? But I'll always remember.

What I cherish are those moments often not captured on film. Those moments aren't centered around a holiday. Those moments happen organically.

The problem is, those moments are more difficult to pull from the memory bank.

I remember the chilly and icy December evening in perfect detail. The four of us were enjoying dinner out on a Friday night. It was cozy. There was a massive fire burning. My wife had those perfect wintery rosy cheeks and a smile that melts me every time.

All of the patrons were bonding in a "ain't life grand" kind of way that can only be attained through the consumption of alcohol. The thin crust pizza was killer. Even the drunks at the bar felt like long-lost friends. You could have filmed a Christmas special here.

It's not easy to truly get in the moment but it was on this night.

The kids were all giggly and whispering and daring me to guess what Mommy just got me for Christmas as we waited for a table to open up. It was one of those moments where I wanted to freeze time; keep the kids at their current age and wrap them all up in a protective coating. Their innocence made me tear then as it does now as I write this.

I eventually coaxed the reveal of the present out of them. It was a Meyer lemon tree that my wife had carefully researched and ordered from a farm in California. They had to let me know at that point so the proper precautions could be taken in terms of maintenance. I agreed that we could plant it the next day, a week or two before December 25.

While Mr. Green Thumb feigned confidence, deep down he panicked because of his lack of citrus tree knowledge. Throw in the added pressure of it being a gift, and I was semi-terrified. But that could be addressed at a later date. The night was too special to ruin with my plant insecurities.

For the next three years, the same cycle of care was applied to the tree. It was carefully brought indoors each autumn where it would pout and drop a bunch of leaves only to rebound just in time when it made its way back outdoors the following spring. Along the way I would get plenty of fragrant flowers but no signs of an actual lemon.

And then one summer, I let out a squeal when I discovered an actual lemon hanging precariously off of a weak and bare branch. The tree itself had seen better days, but the little lemon was enough to keep me inspired heading into the winter.

Once the tree made its way inside the house that fall, I placed it in its usual southern exposure in the kitchen. Except now that we had an actual fruit present, it was time to get way serious. I had a family counting on me to provide for them. If this fruit were not to come to... ahem, fruition...I'd be labeled as a failed provider. These are the times when real men step up and deliver.

It's when they don't fall off of the ladder.

So I purchased a grow light.

I placed the container on a warming blanket.

I fertilized the tree for the first time while it was indoors.

I spritzed the leaves with water regularly.

Within what felt like a day, the lemon started to mature. New growth appeared all over the tree. New flower buds emerged. This one lemon was only the beginning. Soon I'd be the sole provider of citrus in Hunterdon County, New Jersey. I had a "Lemon Guy" t-shirt and website all ready to go.

The only fear was if that little lemon fell off of the painfully weak looking branch. That would be tragic. That would crush us.

I took all necessary precautions to ensure its safety.

All nieces and nephews were banned from even looking at the tree. I couldn't relocate it during family gatherings because it might have knocked the fruit loose so I made sure to turn the tree so the thorniest branches detered all curious onlookers and touchers.

Whenever the tree was outdoors and there was a storm, I shielded the tree from the winds by hiding it behind the grill and other less important plant containers.

The dog was banned from the back deck in summer and the kitchen in winter.

Only I was allowed to water to ensure the little bugger wasn't jarred from the branch.

It took almost a year for the fruit to ripen to maturity. That tiny green fruit evolved to a handsome yellow lemon. I no longer had to argue with those who were convinced it was a lime instead of an unripe lemon.

The timing of the fruit removal could not have ended up better.

On my son's twelfth birthday, I gently pulled the fruit from the branch so we could now proceed with consuming it.

At first, it had been a challenge to determine how best to enjoy it. It had to be special and ceremonious with a lot of pomp and circumstance. We needed to do it right.

Do we all get a quarter of it and simply eat it? I was game but no one else was on board.

Do we use it in a cocktail? Not a bad idea but social services would take the kids if they participated.

Maybe we each take our one-fourth lemon and do whatever the hell we want to with it?

When my son's birthday arrived, the answer became obvious. We were having some family over and had decided to break the bank and serve lobster rolls, one of his personal favorites. While we slaved away at the party prep, my son was chilling, drinking a lemon soda.

I commented first on how he should be helping (bad parenting alert) and then on how much he truly loves all things lemon flavored.

True story: my wife craved and was obsessed with citrus when she was pregnant with my son. Lemonade, lemon ice, lime cookies, and orange juice were all a part of her daily diet. And no lie, from the day he was born and could eat regular foods, my son loved everything lemon flavored. There has to be a connection here.

Ding.

I ran back into the house and consulted with my wife. We had the plan in place.

Out came the lemon and we cut it in half. Looking good and thank the Lord, lemon-like. I then cut it into quarters.

One quarter was eaten by yours truly (delicious).

The family then agreed that the remaining three quarters should be squeezed into a pot.

A pot full of delicious butter.

Butter that would be used for the lobsters.

The lobster rolls were a huge hit and to this day, the best I've ever had. That fresh and homegrown lemon juice made all the difference in the world.

Our special fruit was used for a special kid on his special day.

Hey Hallmark, I've got a commercial idea for you. Call my agent.

Postscript: The following year we had close to 10 to 12 lemons appear on the tree. I stayed on top of all of the necessary steps to ensure their success. The lemons were huge and beautifully yellow, and I honestly thought that I had the magic touch. The "Lemon Guy" dream was becoming a reality.

We cut the first one open the summer of '15 and the rind was almost a half-inch thick. The lemon closely resembled a weird non-lemon. One tiny bite of the pulp and I knew the entire batch was a waste. I proceeded to cut them all and they were all the same: odd and not remotely edible.

The tree died in the winter of 2016 and I've sworn off container-grown fruit trees for good.

That one delicious lemon from the year before became a story of legend and still is to this day.

> *Chew on this:* Passions are contagious. Sharing them with others can inspire them to do bigger and better things.

CHAPTER 28

CASEY

If there are no dogs in Heaven, then when I die I want to go where they went.

—Will Rogers

It's 5:18 a.m. and Casey is barking at the bottom of the stairs. At 15 years old, she doesn't have the strength, or the desire, to run up the stairs to announce that she needs to pee. She discovered a few years back that dancing on the hardwood floor in the foyer was an efficient means to communicate her needs. The sound easily echoes into our bedroom and acts as our morning alarm. While I don't always welcome it with a smile, I eventually smile and understand that it is a blessing to still have Casey, our yellow Labrador, after 15 years.

That's rare.

And I also understand that she owns an elderly dog's weak bladder.

On this morning though, she is up two hours earlier than normal. That has rarely happened over the past few years. I'm only slightly concerned and announce to her that I'm coming.

Why I announce my intentions is still a mystery. Casey

has been deaf for two years running. I may be in denial or deep down I believe she can still pick up on the message in her secret dog way. We now only communicate through hand motions.

I jump out of bed, toss on a sweatshirt, walk down the stairs, attach her leash, and we head outside. As I wait for Casey to take care of business, I am incapable of thought, and my eyes may not even be open. All I keep dreaming about is returning to my warm bed and maybe another two hours of sleep. This is a common practice on weekends.

After five minutes I realize Casey has no interest in squatting. She is only interested in smelling the scents left behind by the deer and rabbits from the night before. I eventually coerce her into coming back inside so she can enjoy her breakfast, but I'm still confused as to why she won't pee. Something is off.

I head over to her food bowl and throw in two scoops. But Casey has no interest in eating. That never happens. She has voraciously eaten every meal since 1999. I walk over to her so we can have a chat and then realize what's going on.

My cold and bare feet are drenched.

Now I know why she never did #1 outside.

She did #1 inside.

I grab a bunch of paper towels, some Clorox wipes, and begin to clean up. I am now officially awake for the day, no more thoughts of a return trip to my warm and inviting bed.

Ten minutes later and we're as good as new. Casey is

no longer worried about the pee barrier to her food bowl and is chowing down. Normalcy has returned, other than the fact that I'm washing my feet in the bathtub. It's all a small price to pay for this dog who has been with us for a decade and a half.

Since I am now up for the day, I make a pot of coffee and hop on my laptop. Casey and I catch up on our favorite websites as the sun rises. I love this dog, but I am tired.

A few minutes in, Casey puts her head on my lap, the universal sign that she wants something from me. Since there are no treats in sight and I know she isn't a coffee fan, I can only assume that she is now in need of pee #2.

I grab her leash, once again, and my heavenly black coffee and we head outside.

Similar to before, she refuses to pee. I'm frustrated and tired and if I'm being honest, a tad bit sick of her shenanigans. I am willing to wait her out because I don't want to do this again.

Casey then pulls me with strength she hasn't displayed in a long time, like the young puppy who could drag me around as if I was water skiing. I'm confused yet thankful that she still has this level of energy in her.

I oblige her pulling and we end up on the driveway.

And there I see the greatest display of a "morning garden" that I've ever seen in person.

It looks like we are in the middle of a movie set.

The sun is shining down on all of the blooming ornamental grasses and they all look like they are laced with crystals.

It hurts to stare at them for longer than a few seconds. But holy shit is it a gorgeous display.

I glance back at Casey and she appears to have a grin on her face with her arms crossed as if to say, "Kind of beautiful, isn't it?"

She never did pee.

Casey passed exactly two months later. She died on December 13, 2014—12/13/14. We often use it as a password. Just don't tell anyone that.

I remember our last pee outside. I knew it was the last one because we were going to bring her to the vet to put her down right after.

We had so many pee trips together over the years through snow, frost, rain, blinding morning sun, and the stillness of night. In the beginning she would almost pull my arm off. By the end, I had to carry her up the two front steps and she totally ignored the nearby deer.

While it was devastating, we knew that we won the lottery with her. She was there before the first child. She gently engaged both children when they were infants. She spanned three presidents. She swam at the lake until she couldn't stand.

She gave us a lifetime of memories.

I'll always believe she intended to bring me outside that magical autumn morning at just the perfect time.

I'm a cynical bastard but you'll never convince me otherwise.

I use the photos of the ornamental grasses from that morning to sell readers and family and friends on their fall and winter beauty.

Thanks, Casey.

> **Chew on this:** It's all about gratitude. Casey lived 15 healthy years and that's unheard of for a Labrador Retriever. Gratitude fosters well-being. Start a gratitude journal and jot down what you're thankful for each day. Focus on the positives in your life and it can impact your happiness.

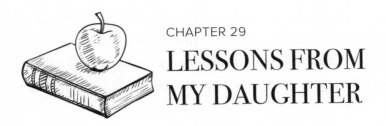

CHAPTER 29

LESSONS FROM MY DAUGHTER

Children see magic because they look for it.

—Christopher Moore

"Do we have any groups of two?"

I'm going to pretend that I don't hear him by staring intently into my phone.

"Is anyone riding with only two?"

Stare harder, John.

"If there is anybody in line with only two in their party, you can jump the line and get on this ride right now."

"We're only two," she yells.

Shit.

I don't want to navigate through these 100 people in line. There are kids dangling from the railings. There are teenagers smacking each other. That dude with the face tattoo is disturbing. I don't want to interrupt conversations while bumping into these sweaty people. The width of this entry line is already making me claustrophobic.

I was content slowly making our way to the front of the line for this roller coaster ride, but not her.

These thoughts don't exist anywhere within her.

Who is this girl I call daughter?

I would sign a document right here and now if it

guaranteed that I could go unnoticed for the remainder of my time on this planet. I think my wife and son would do the same. It's not that we're completely anti-social or hardcore introverts, we just prefer not to have the spotlight shine on us at any point.

But my daughter, she's very different.

It's not that she craves that spotlight as much as she doesn't give two fucks if that light shines on her from time to time. She knows what she wants and has tunnel vision when it comes to getting it.

She wanted to maximize "Dad and Daughter Day" at the amusement park that summer and if that means uncomfortably jumping a line, so be it.

I don't want her to be like me. I want her to grab life by the throat and squeeze every inch of thrill out of it. I don't want others to dictate her happiness. I want her to always be moving forward.

I need to stay out of her way.

My daughter's favorite show has always been *Phineas and Ferb*. It's a Disney Channel cartoon where two brothers spend their summer vacation dreaming up largescale and ridiculous ideas and then actually see them to fruition.

They travel back in time via a time machine and visit the dinosaurs. They create their own beach. They construct a roller coaster in their backyard.

Super silly kid stuff, but my daughter views it differently.

I watch her when she watches it. She dreams big right along with the characters but through a realistic lens. She has asked me on more than one occasion if it's possible to build our own roller coaster. Not in a cute "aw" way but more like, "I'm serious here, Dad. Why can't we?"

I found one of her Google searches that sums it up beautifully:

"Most realistic things built by Phineas & Ferb"

It made me cry.

"No" is never accepted as the first answer. She doesn't settle. She needs to explore for herself first. She just needs to do.

I need to stay out of her way.

While at Knoebels Amusement Resort in Elysburg, Pennsylvania, we rode the log flume six times over the course of 24 hours. Each time I felt great relief when we hit the bottom of the final steep drop.

Fears of a malfunctioning log could be suppressed again. Disturbing images of falling disappeared as we slowly floated back to the starting point of the ride. It was fun for me but more out of survival than enjoyable adrenaline rush.

As we slowly made our way to the end of the ride for the last time, my daughter turned around, looked at me, and said, "Enjoy these last moments because technically we're still on the log flume." My thoughts had already turned to the long ride home, whether or not I should stop for gas early in the trip, and the work I left hanging on Friday.

I need to stay out of her way.

Ever since I can remember, I've maintained this need to keep an inner balance: never too high and never too low. I don't know where it stems from, but only later in life have I even acknowledged its existence. It might sound like a positive way to go about living your life but I'm learning that it really isn't.

Yes, I've always managed not to get too low when life throws something negative my way. My mantra of "it could always be worse" has helped me keep my sanity. I've also been able to share that sentiment with those close to me and I think it has helped them.

You think this is bad, what about [fill in the blank] who just found out [fill in the blank].

But with that comes an inability to truly embrace the great moments. I never allow myself to get too high or too happy in fear of being let down when that great moment dissipates. It's been a weird dance with karma my entire life. In an odd way, I feel like I could jinx that great moment if I become too caught up in its enjoyment.

Yes, it's overanalysis at its finest, and I hate it.

And it extends to my garden as well.

But it wasn't until my therapist pointed out the parallel that it even crossed my mind.

I want to be my daughter as a gardener. She would no doubt enjoy letting the garden run wild. I too want it to be fun and out of control and whimsical. I really do. The gardens I enjoy most are those that are chaotic and natural and not defined by strict guidelines.

But I'm still me in the garden. I prefer control. I prefer that every plant remain within its boundaries. I prefer order. Not too unlike the boy who loved a lawn free of leaves, with perfect edges and beds filled with mulch.

Yet I despise a formal garden where order is the name

of the game. So I'm trying to operate somewhere in the middle of both extremes. I believe controlled chaos in the garden is my perfect compromise. I just need to determine the best means for me to move closer to the chaos side.

I'm working on myself. I'm meditating, I'm reading, and I'm opening my mind to spirituality. I'm trying to get better at letting go and handing over the reins. I'm trying to live in the moment.

I'm trying to be okay with that random coneflower that popped up out of nowhere. I'm trying to be okay with that overgrown spirea shrub. I'm trying to be okay with a few weeds here and there.

Maybe progress starts with the garden.

Maybe progress starts between my two ears.

Maybe it's a little of both.

Maybe I'll just allow it to play out and surrender control.

Maybe I'll just follow my daughter's lead.

Chew on this: Do you look to your children for inspiration? They are part you, yet not you but they can educate you on you. I hope you made sense of that prior sentence. It's killer advice.

WRITE

CHAPTER 30

EMAIL

There is nothing in the world so irresistibly contagious as laughter and good humor.

—Charles Dickens

When I entered the workforce in 1995, email didn't exist at my company. Scratch that, there was some bizarre communication mechanism we could only use internally, but we didn't call it email. I remember a black screen and blinking green dots and having to enter a strange code just to initiate a message. I don't think the message could exceed 45 characters. But even with those limitations we still found it to be cutting edge.

And like twentysomethings are wont to do, we sent goofy messages to one another just so we could secretly peek over the cubicle walls and watch the others laugh. It was only a step up from the likes of Beavis and Butthead.

By 1997, we had email, the real deal. It was Lotus Notes from IBM and it was groundbreaking. We could easily communicate with coworkers across the country and reconnect with high school friends on the sly. For those of us who despised speaking on the telephone, this was heaven.

Plus there was a written trail of proof for all business matters that could be referenced at a later date if need be.

I liked that.

Yes, I went through an "email forwarding" stage like everyone else and may have participated in a chain mail or ten. I, too, feared ten years of bad luck and also thought Bill Gates would be sending me $100,000 in the mail. You did this too, and you know it. We all did.

But more than anything else, I loved email as a means to bring people together. Email as a means to break down walls at work. Email as super functional yet entertaining.

Once email became the norm at work, it didn't take long for "those" coworkers to flex their corporate-speak muscles. It was bad enough to have to hear it on a conference call, or in the cafeteria, but in writing it pained that much more.

"I want to ensure that we've taken the holistic view of this synergistic initiative and I ask that we leverage the delta we derived during yesterday's deep dive meeting. If we can eliminate the low hanging fruit we can then proceed with our blamestorming session."

Holy yuck. Please stop.

Fortunately we had like-minded folks like myself who could speak in simple and authentic terms.

"Let's make sure we thought this through, eh?"

We felt a bond in keeping it real. We came together in the name of no BS. We took turns forwarding these hideous emails to one another where we translated the babbling into normal-speak. We made one another laugh.

The only concern was to make sure we forwarded the emails to one another and didn't mistakenly "Reply All."

A "Reply All" would include the original email and its author in our responses so they would then be privy to our mocking. I saw it happen a few times and it was awkward times ten.

I mastered another skill during this time of email and it's one I'm still proud of to this day because I still do it. I became really good at diffusing chaos. I enjoyed playing the role of calming influence.

While everyone panicked and bounced off of their gray cubicle walls and email conversations became an instant fire drill, I found a way to slickly talk everyone off the ledge while at the same time acknowledging there was work to get done.

"I realize the fact that our website has a misspelling is a big deal and that is the equivalent of performing open heart surgery..."

"Please allow me to cry first before I address that customer issue..."

"Before we start the meeting, I have something we must discuss first. What the hell happened on Lost *last night? Crazy weird, right?"*

Of course, I was always careful to ensure I knew exactly who was on the email distribution list. I kept my audiences small and I limited it only to those I knew I could trust.

And guess what? We kicked ass in every situation. We got the work done. We made our customers happy and we exceeded their mutha f'n expectations. If it meant first taking a breath and gathering ourselves through well-timed and much-needed humor, so be it. It worked, and it became our go-to method for problem resolution.

I never really figured out how to add this "skill" to my resume so if you have an idea for a proper description, please send me an email.

Here's a little tidbit I've never told anyone: I absolutely loved entertaining my coworkers with my email prowess. I lived to make them laugh at the wrong time. I treated my email as performance art. It was my version of performing stand-up.

I lived to set them up with what looked like a serious email, before I dropped the humor on them. I made it my mission to slow things down first before we sped up.

Humor can do that.

I don't think it's too much of a stretch to say that this was my love of writing peeking its head out. Sure it was only few sentences at a time, but I crafted each of those sentences very carefully. I worked hard at my timing and enjoyed displaying just the slightest amount of vulnerability. And I soaked in the positive feedback.

An "LOL" meant a lot back then; it wasn't a throwaway like it is today.

An "OMG" was even better.

But nothing beat "you are too funny."

Quick aside: If you have a moment, Google "Tucker Max email" and you'll see how he became a bestselling author as the direct result of emails he sent to his friends. His writing started there as well.

You're welcome.

To my old coworkers: Yes, I made you laugh at times when it was most needed, but it also indirectly led to the resolution of a problem.

It allowed you to better focus on the task at hand.

It is and will always be a viable strategy.

If you remember me for anything, remember me for this.

Chew on this: Take an inventory of your natural talents. Put them into practice as often as you can. I best communicate through the written word so I used that as my means for problem solving at work.

194

CHAPTER 31

THE BLOG

There is nothing to writing. All you do is sit down at a typewriter and bleed.

—Ernest Hemingway

It all started so innocently.

It was a cold weeknight evening in February 2010 and my wife and I were watching the show *Lost*. I was obsessed with the show, watching each episode multiple times and then taking to the *Lost* message boards to discuss theories and to speculate where the story was going. I had to watch on my my laptop so I could easily access the Internet should an Easter egg be dropped during an episode.

On this particular evening, it was a dull episode and my mind started to wander. I was surfing the web and veering off into garden planning. Spring was just weeks away and I had to ensure that I had accounted for all of my online orders and where they could potentially be sited.

Somewhere along the way I stumbled on to the blogging site "Blogger" and started to play around. Before long I had chosen a template, a theme, and had a temporary title for a blog, "The King of Garden Failures."

I may have mentioned this already so I apologize for repeating it: I'm a big fan of self-deprecation. I'm also a fan of authenticity. The two go hand in hand; hence the reasoning behind the not-so-positive blog title. I was truly failing a ton in my garden.

I had given some thought to starting a garden blog prior to this. I wanted it to be a realistic look at the pains and failures of gardening, which seemed to be ignored by most writers. It will never be all pretty all the time. I wanted real and thought real could stand out in a crowd of the too pretty garden blogs, which were exploding all over the internet at that time.

I wrote my first blog post that night. It was two paragraphs long and it focused on my frustration with understanding garden design.

I hit "Submit" on the post and left it at that. I had no plans from there.

The next day I awoke with odd vigor to see this blog thing through. I felt energized after only one post and felt energized by allowing it to live where the world could see it. Even if in reality no one would knew it was there.

I immediately changed the name to "The Obsessive Neurotic Gardener." That name felt more fun and catchy and 100 percent me.

After that initial post, I informed no one, other than my wife, of its existence. I didn't want any courtesy reads and feel-like-you-have-to comments. I wanted to build it from the soil up and I felt no rush to build an audience. I could work out the kinks without anyone noticing.

I began to write regularly on the blog although "write" may be a stretch. It was more of a ramble, more of a confessional style that defied all that we learn in Writing 101.

After a few months of mostly dreadful and incoherent posts, I realized I was missing out by not placing photos within these posts. Photos are everything with a garden (duh). It's one thing to talk about a plant, it's another thing to show a photo that perfectly outlines your point.

I took hundreds of photos at a time. I experimented with lighting and with angles. The early pics were admittedly bad but it didn't take long before I taught myself how to do it right. It changed the look and feel of the blog immediately and allowed me to express another creative side that had never been revealed.

Once I had a rhythm with my posts and corresponding photos, I took the plunge and started sharing the posts on Facebook. Then I went on a Facebook friending spree making sure anyone I ever crossed paths with was a "friend."

This then extended to anyone who gave even the slightest indication that they liked plants. Friend request sent, no questions asked. It didn't matter if you were from the U.S. or Prague. We would unite in our love of gardening.

My new circle was established and all would happily consume my writing. I had a fearlessness that I had never felt before. I was ready to share my writing with the world.

Things started to get interesting quickly. The traffic to the blog increased as a result of the Facebook shares, which was great. It kept me on my toes knowing there were actual eyes on it.

I welcomed the escape and the chance for expression. When reader comments started to slowly filter in I became addicted. This is what I envisioned back in 1990 when I entered college and had dreams of writing professionally. It only took me twenty years to get the mojo back.

Fast forward to today and I've written 1,500-plus posts solely about my gardening experiences. I have never gone longer than a week without posting. At one point I was writing a post five days a week without fail.

What started as a whim became a real thing.

Recognition from those who read the blog led to very cool opportunities.

I have had my garden and my writing featured on the *Fine Gardening* website multiple times.

I was featured in *Birds & Blooms* magazine. I have close to twenty copies of it at home if you're interested.

I won the best blogger award in my county and attended a red carpet event with my wife. It felt goofy yet fun.

I was asked to be on a local gardening radio show. I immediately felt comfortable speaking into a microphone. I even felt a bit cocky with it. This was where I belonged. The performer emerged again.

I've since signed on to be a semi-regular cohost on that same show.

I'm super proud that to this day, the blog hasn't strayed from its initial vision. I wanted to document rather than overtly inform. I wanted a record of my learning. I wanted a record of my evolving. It was always to be about the journey and not about bravado or pretending to be an expert.

I've always been honest about my struggles and have happily shared photos of what I did wrong and what that can look like in the garden.

I've never been preachy or told readers what to do or how to do it. Here's what I did, here's what worked, here's what didn't work, take with it what you will.

I've never sold gardening as easy. In fact, I like to remind readers that it's really hard. And we like it that way because that provides deeper fulfillment in the long run. It's a marathon and not a sprint. The process of building the garden is what stimulates us, not the results.

From a personal development point of view, choosing to start this blog was the greatest decision I've ever made. I had long since abandoned my love of writing before the blog began; somewhere along the way I got lost.

I thank my lucky stars that I rediscovered it.

I'm more open when writing and more willing to be honest and forthright. I'm at my funniest when I'm writing. I think I can entertain through my words.

It all started slowly with my creative emails at work.

It gained steam as I lived on the gardening forums and shared my garden with others.

But it really took off through some initial rambling about my love of plants.

Those ramblings paid off.

> ***Chew on this:*** What's preventing you from taking the first step? Start small, forget about perfection and don't wait for the "right time."

CHAPTER 32

THE WRITER'S CONFERENCE

The further you get away from yourself, the more challenging it is. Not to be in your comfort zone is great fun.

—Benedict Cumberbatch

I'll start this story off with a question.

Would you attend a conference that includes the best of the best in your field, profession, hobby, and so forth if you were only six months into being a part of said field, profession, hobby, and so on?

For me the answer is a definitive "no" like 98.3 percent of the time.

But back in the late summer of 2010, some strange being took over my body and committed to attending the Garden Writer's Association conference in Dallas, Texas.

I don't know who this being was but I wouldn't mind being able to recall he or she with the snap of a finger.

This being had guts.

This being was fearless.

This being not only threw caution to the wind but kicked caution relentlessly after the wind blew it to the ground.

Yes, I may be pouring it on a little thick, but this was so out of character for me. I'd never allowed myself to be uncomfortable. I'd never put myself in a situation where I could be outed as a fraud. I'd never exposed myself to the unknown.

Yet there I was boarding a plane in Philadelphia, Pennsylvania, as if I were an editor at *Fine Gardening* magazine.

I remember telling myself: *I must have a legitimate passion for this gardening thing if I'm so willing to put myself in harm's way.*

I'm going to become preachy for a brief moment. I feel very strongly about what I'm about to say, well, actually write, unless this is an audio book and if this is an audio book, wow, go me!

Do what makes you uncomfortable.

Face those fears head on.

It's a cliché yes, but there's a reason it became a cliché. They're true and not easy to overcome.

While attending a writer's conference may not equate to singing a solo in Times Square in your skivvies, it still had elements that terrified me: meeting strangers, dining with strangers, exchanging business cards, and attempting to explain why a newbie blogger would attend a conference.

And I ended up loving the fact that I fought through the fear and came out okay on the other side.

Each interaction was a win.

I found myself gaining momentum as I came out of my shell. I met a couple who were both photographers and lived in the town where I grew up. They supported my being there. They praised my fearlessness. They introduced me to the president of the Garden Writer's Association (GWA) who ultimately asked me to write a piece on being a first-timer at the conference.

Surviving a meal without embarrassing myself was a win. Don't laugh, but I mastered, *"Is anyone sitting here? What do you do?"* That's a normal course of conversation for most but not for me. I met a newspaper editor during a lunch who provided me with invaluable lessons on how to promote my work.

Chatting up a way more accomplished writer on a bus ride was a win. A book editor sat next to me on a ride to a public garden. She sat and listened to me explain "blogging." She questioned the integrity of a blog and laughed it off as a fad. She deemed all blogs not to be credible. That happily pissed me off and pushed me forward even more.

Mimicking professional photographers during public garden tours was a win. I still use that knowledge when in my own garden today.

Getting free plants was a win. I taught myself how to get them home, while traveling across the country on a plane, without them dying.

Visiting a wild and chaotic garden was a huge win. I fell in love with its style and do my best to copy that in my own garden, even with my nagging OCD tendencies.

Willingly and happily paying attention to each and every speaker was a win. I had fallen asleep at least once at every other conference I had ever attended up until that point. It's amazing what happens when you're in your element, hanging with the right people and listening to topics that are stimulating to your core.

Add up all those wins and I had, like, a lot of wins.

The courage I gained from attending a conference I had no right to be at gave me the courage to keep writing and to be fearless in putting it out to the world. That, in turn, provided the courage to try anything, be it in the garden or with writing.

A cautious gardener and cautious writer aren't very interesting.

Chew on this: Force yourself out of your comfort zone. That is where the breakthroughs occur. People I met at this conference helped me create the book you are currently reading.

CHAPTER 33

SPRING TRAINING

Baseball is like church. Many attend, few understand.

—Leo Durocher

The Markowski family bleeds blue and orange for our beloved New York Mets. That darn baseball team dominates our thoughts and infiltrates our conversations from February through October each and every year. We never miss a game on TV and if we can't watch them, rest assured we'll listen to them on the radio.

My wife and I both come from a long line of Mets fans. I'm not sure she would have said "I do" if I rooted for the Yankees. And it would have made for awful holidays and Sunday dinners. Thankfully we never had to worry.

For years now, we've made the trip south to Port St. Lucie, Florida, to watch our Mets practice during the time that is known as Spring Training or as I like to call it, "F the Winter."

Yes, it's an escape from the dreaded wintery conditions here in the northeastern U.S. Yes, it's a chance to get away on a mini-vacation.

But it's really so much more than that.

Watching grown men play a game a few hours each

morning may be for the diehard baseball fan only, but I'm here to wave the banner and inform you that it runs deeper.

I find Spring Training to be the ultimate inspiration for writing. It is the first non-gardening topic I ever covered on my blog. I write a daily summary of the day's events on my laptop in the hotel room later that night. Not to toot my own horn (too late) but readers beg for these recaps every year.

I find Spring Training stokes my passion for photography. I have captured action shots that have been used by other websites. I have blown up Instagram with candid photos of players in action or goofing around on the diamond.

I find it to be family bonding at its finest.

I find it to be an annual reunion of like-minded fans, all of whom cannot wait to talk of anything but baseball for a few days each February.

And as I put my deeper-thinking baseball cap on, I realized that the joy of Spring Training extends beyond the baseball field. The reasons why I vow to trek south each and every February for the rest of eternity is not only about baseball. All of the baseball metaphors can be applied to any other profession, hobby, passion, or life calling.

I know I'm a better gardener and a better writer because of the days I spend watching and observing these athletes.

Think I'm crazy? Allow me to explain.

A fresh start

Every team is undefeated when Spring Training starts. Every player has another chance to prove himself. Spring Training is littered with redemption stories; players giving it one last shot, holding on to one last hope to fulfill their childhood dreams. If they work hard enough and they catch a break, maybe this is the year it all comes to fruition.

I look at my garden the same way each spring, as a new beginning and another chance to pull together something special. There is nothing but promise, at least until that first weed appears or that shrub didn't survive the winter.

Watching "experts" in their element doing what they love

Yes, most players are making millions to play a silly game. Yes, they don't have a real "job." But there's something inspiring just watching a Major League Baseball player have a catch with another Major League Baseball player. You can still see the Little Leaguer in them. You can see the smiles on their faces as they toss that rawhide around. They've been here many times before and yet they still enjoy the simple thrill of tossing a baseball back and forth.

Watching players outside of the limelight

The New York Mets spring training complex is very understated. It looks more like a high school than it does the major leagues. And I love that. It humanizes the players; they pull into the parking lot each morning without scores of reporters or hundreds of screaming fans. It reduces the scene down to its basics. It's simple baseball minus the typical hoopla. It makes me appreciate the purity of the game, which is lost throughout a normal baseball season.

Watch players operate outside of a game situation

There is no game to get pumped up for. There are no silly pre-game superstitions or a refusal to speak to anyone while the players get primed for that day's game. There is laughter and there is joking around. You get to see players reconnect after a winter apart. You spot the special bonds and special friendships among certain players. It is relaxed, and it is pressure free. It is the calm before the Major League Baseball season.

You can appreciate their skill level up close and personal

These are the top performers in their field. Thousands have tried and failed. These are the ones who have survived, who have persevered, and who have defeated the odds. They throw with ease. They run effortlessly. They hit a tiny ball with a wooden stick 500 feet without breaking a sweat. It is a specialized skill, one a bystander at Spring Training can see up close and personal. It is a thrill to watch live and it is inspiring.

Watching millionaires put in the time and effort to be the best they can be

If you look closely enough, you can see the effort players are putting in to get their bodies and minds in shape. It's awesome to be able to see it all start from the beginning before the games commence. Yes, there is enormous natural ability on display, but there is also a need to work one's ass off. That is fun to watch play out. That makes the success stories that much more special, to say you've been there from the beginning.

Reverting back to childhood

As you know, I collected baseball cards. I watched endless hours of baseball. I played the game and tried to emulate my favorite players.

As soon as I enter that first practice, it all comes rushing back in one fell swoop.

The emotion is palpable, and I can't get enough of it.

Watching my son

My son collects baseball cards. My son has an enormous autograph collection, most of them secured while we've been at Spring Training. I can watch him operate all day. That youthful exuberance, even as he ages through his teens, when one of his favorite players walks from his car to sign for him makes the trip worth it.

> **Chew on this:** Study the best of the best in your field
> of interest, and do what they do. Educate yourself on
> what they do behind the scenes.

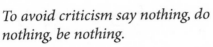

CRITICISM

*To avoid criticism say nothing, do
nothing, be nothing.*

—Elbert Hubbard

After a few years of writing the blog, I got an itch to do
something different. I'd still write because I'll never stop
again; I just wanted to try something new.

Some people suggested I write a book. I immediately
scoffed, knowing I'd never have the time to dedicate to
an undertaking like that. I also knew I had no authority
to be an authority on any gardening topic. Those who
author gardening books are true experts who garden and
write full-time and have done so for decades. I'd have
nothing new, educational, or interesting to bring to the
table.

(Yes, I've since written two books including the one
you're holding, but you get the point.)

I had dabbled a bit in creating garden videos for
YouTube and considered dedicating my time to that
medium. That idea lasted about a week when I realized
gardening videos, at least the type I was trying to create,
were pleasantly boring and hard as hell to create on my
own. I was shaky, monotone, and dull as I tried to dazzle
the viewers with how riveting it can be to cut back an

ornamental grass in spring.

At this same time, podcasts were becoming all the rage. I had actually been a guest on a few of them. I'm not sure what prompted the hosts to invite me but who was I to turn down the opportunity? It wasn't my fault when people subsequently fell asleep listening to two gardeners talk about their gardens.

The hosts were great, and for those of us who reside in the niche that is gardening, the podcasts were interesting and educational.

So why not join them? Why not jump into the world of hosting a podcast myself?

After extensive research, I found a company that allowed me to record podcasts for free. The only stipulation was that I'd have to record them after 11 p.m., during their downtime. Who wouldn't want to join an inexperienced and awkward host while the clock struck midnight?

As expected, I was bad at the beginning. Luckily I invited guests who were gardening friends so they were incredibly patient and willing to work with me as I ironed out the wrinkles. And by the way, "gardening people" are the greatest people on earth. It's true, look it up. They are the kindest folk on the planet.

As time wore on, I got better and more comfortable and even secured some killer guests.

Do you know Joe Lamp'l from *Growing a Greener World?* I interviewed him.

Do you know Erica Glasener from HGTV's *A Gardener's Diary?* I interviewed her.

It's funny; sometimes all you need to do is ask. I reached

them directly via social media, and they didn't hesitate to say "yes." That's a big life lesson right there, take note.

Just as I was hitting my groove, or so I thought, I read this comment on Apple iTunes from a listener:

"Great guests, but the host has too long of awkward pauses. You can tell the guests notice it as well. It's uncomfortable to listen to. You should be asking more garden-related topics and less production and career path questions."

Okay then.

I never recorded another podcast after reading this.

One negative comment and I retired from podcasting.

How's that for perseverance?

Some of you, and I emphasize "some," may have read my first book, *Perennials Through the Seasons.* Thanks, by the way, if I never told you that.

I came up with the concept in 2016 and started writing it soon after. I pitched it to all of the publishers who published gardening books and all politely declined. I understood. I was a newbie and the only "brand" I could offer was my blog. They needed to know I could sell a book based on my reputation, and I couldn't prove that.

So I gave up.

But then I didn't.

Self-publishing gives everyone an opportunity to be an author and while it can be debated that it may not be a good thing, I cherished the chance. I told myself I would see it through. I would put in the full effort and do it all myself: the writing, the editing, the layout, the cover, the marketing. I would not care how many books I'd sell. I wanted to get it done. I wanted to learn and enjoy the process.

And on April 12, 2017, I did it.

The book was released.

I haven't sold many books, and I still don't care.

I've promoted it and enjoyed it the entire time.

I wrote the first book so I could get to the second book.

As Elizabeth Gilbert once told me (well not me directly, it was in *Big Magic*): *"Done is better than good."*

There have been decent reviews on Amazon and I know that those are my loyal blog readers. I so appreciate them but also understand that their comments aren't the best gauge as to the quality of the book.

One review stands out. It was the lowest rated and the most honest. It was also the most negative. Feel free to check it out on Amazon right now for full effect.

My first reaction was, *"I can't find your book on Amazon, dude. Remind me where I can find it again?"*

My next reaction was this book you are holding right now.

Drops mic.

Chew on this: It's crucial to understand the difference between constructive criticism and destructive criticism. The former fosters growth and the latter serves no purpose.

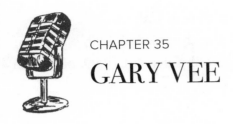

CHAPTER 35

GARY VEE

Even if your ambitions are huge, start slow, start small, build gradually, build smart.

—Gary Vaynerchuk

I love my commute to work. Those 45 minutes in the morning give me a chance to inhale black coffee, clear the cobwebs, and to slowly and methodically get inspired. That inspiration typically comes from a podcast. The subjects can vary and range from comedy to meditation to stoking creativity. Even if I lived three minutes from the office, I'd drive in circles until I was good and ready to set foot in the building.

The drive home at night is to unwind. It's for me and only me. I cherish that alone time, and I cherish the opportunity to forget about the day through getting lost in Pearl Jam or Radiohead. I'll only answer the phone if it's my wife.

It wasn't always this way. I used to blast music just to wake my lazy butt up. Or I'd listen to sports talk radio and yell at the host when he was wrong. Or I'd just zone out. I never considered going deeper than that.

I wasn't a self-help guy. I found it all to be silly, repetitive, and ultimately a scam. I never found screaming with empty promises appealing.

You should set goals, blah blah blah.

You should create a dream board, blah blah blah.

You should buy my e-book for just $79.99, blah blah blah.

No thank you.

One April evening in 2016 (if I haven't told you already, I have quite the memory, especially when it comes to dates) my wife and I were on our dueling laptops when she stumbled across this dude's audio recording on Twitter and played it out loud.

At first I chuckled. Who's this nut job? Why is he so fiery?

He sounded different. He sounded real. He was, in fact, nuts, in a good way. He was from Jersey. He was my age. He cursed a lot.

And apparently he'd been massively successful. He kept harping on his desire to someday buy his favorite NFL team, the New York Jets.

His name is Gary Vaynerchuk, or Gary Vee to those of us in the know.

I had a full-blown man crush.

Here are just a few of his quotes that captivated me:

If you live for the weekends and vacations, your sh*t is broken.
Stop doing sh*t you hate.
F*ck "you're gonna."
Ideas are sh*t.

Mind blown.

I know what you're thinking, groundbreaking, right?

You're blown away by the depth of meaning, right?

Here's the thing: He spoke to me. He lit a fire under me. He worked for me. It wasn't so much what he said as it was how he said it.

It was if he knew how to break through my preconceived notions of a self-help guru and got right to the point. He defied the stereotype of the slick salesman. He wasn't trying to sell me anything. I felt like—gulp—he actually cared.

And I'm selling him way short with just showing the profanity laced quotes. Other things he said (and I'm paraphrasing) that left a mark:

"If you love Wiffle Ball, become the world's most informed and passionate Wiffle Ball blogger."

"Document. Don't create. Just because you're documenting doesn't mean you're not creating content."

"Bet on your strengths. It's an underrated business strategy in a world where so many people are obsessed with fixing their weaknesses they give short shrift to the skills they were born with."

GV entered my world at the perfect time. I was creatively stuck after years writing on the blog. Podcasting didn't work for me. I wanted to expand my writing outside of plants. But I didn't know what to do next. I had been spending months lost inside my head, dreaming up ideas but doing nothing about it.

All GV had to say was "Ideas are sh*t," and I was listening.

I read his book *Crush It!* in one night. I listened to every episode of "Ask Gary Vee" on YouTube. I followed him on all forms of social media.

I sent him an email and he responded. I even tried to get a job working for him.

I may have been a bit too much of a fanboy, but what set GV apart from all of the others was that he provided specific advice and specific ways to execute.

He's the reason why I found *Medium*, the online publishing platform. I've been writing on that site for years now and have enjoyed success with my non-gardening writing. It's opened doors to other writing opportunities. I'm even making some real cash.

I'm doing my best to remember "just do." (I left out the "it" so Nike won't sue me although that would be great book publicity. But they would drain me through lawyers' fees and that wouldn't be fun.)

I used that tenet to write my first book.

I used it to write this book.

I'll use it for book #3 and whatever else follows.

The right voice at the right time can make all the difference in the world.

The ironic thing is that I don't listen to Gary Vee all that much of late. He would be proud of that. He pushes that. He wants us all spending more time doing and spending less time listening and thinking.

> *Chew on this:* Ideas really are kind of worthless unless you take action.

CHAPTER 36

GOING VIRAL

Life is a long lesson in humility.

—J.M. Barrie

After years of writing about my garden on the blog and dabbling in videos and podcasting, I had a burning desire to start writing about anything but gardening. I needed a foil. I wanted to share my thoughts on family. I wanted to dive into the joys and pains of aging. I wanted to write about baseball. I wanted the freedom to write about anything.

As you just read, Gary Vaynerchuk pointed me towards *Medium*, and the rest is history.

The beauty of this site is that it provides a writer with a built-in audience. *Medium* attracts a bevy of well-known and impressive authors, but if your story is good and genuine, it will still find a large audience. This wasn't starting a blog from scratch where you have to submit to self-promotion 24/7 just to get a few people to take notice. The readers are already there and they're waiting for your masterpiece.

I spent the first six months writing consistently on the platform. I jumped from topic to topic with the goal of becoming a well-rounded writer. There was a small increase in story "views" as time passed and I gained some followers, but nothing substantial. While I appreciated that *Medium* provided an outlet for me to expand my writing chops, I wasn't finding my audience as expected.

To combat that, I read and consumed everything I could find that offered advice on how to find readers on *Medium*. I became educated on which story topics were more popular than others. I learned that stories that have lists are more likely to be read than those without lists. A catchy title, subtitle, and photo are ways to garner attention. Any post that mentions millennials, technology, or start-ups has a chance to be seen by the many.

If I'm being honest, at the time I wanted nothing more than to know how to game the system. I wanted lots of views and lots of likes. If I could get just one post to go viral, I'd be good to go from there.

I got that viral post soon after.

It came out of nowhere.

My stats page blew up. There were 100 new readers each time I clicked the refresh button. I made it to the *Medium* home page, which meant I was kind of a big deal.

My day had arrived.

The story that went viral didn't take me long to write. I put very little effort into its creation. It was a comparison of life in the 1970s and 1980s versus current day. It was formulated as a conversation between me and my two children after they laughed at me for saying:

"*I taped the show you guys wanted to watch.*"

Their mocking made me curse them for having it so

easy today versus what I went through as a child.

Here's a sample anecdote from the story:

You kids simply text us when baseball practice is over. I used to call collect (I'm not taking the time to explain here) from a pay phone and my parents knew to decline, which meant I was ready to be picked up after basketball practice.

To make it even more fun, I used to make up names like Ben Dover or Seymour Buttz when I made the call just to hear the operator repeat it back to my mom.

It was a true hoot.

The premise of the post was simple but funny. I also riffed on riding in the middle of the front seat of the car without a seat belt, old cable TV boxes, and having to wear super small basketball shorts that left nothing to the imagination.

I assume it struck a chord because so many could relate. It was written as a list with funny photos accompanying each item. It was an easy and light read.

The post went viral for a few weeks. Up until that point, my stories never attracted more than a few hundred readers. This article was read by thousands after only a day. I was obsessed with the numbers for days, checking my phone every five minutes.

I was asked for permission to allow it to appear on a number of other sites. I received an endless parade of comments and emails with people sharing similar stories of their own.

An Australian news agency ran it as a top story on their blog and paid me handsomely for the rights to share it.

The day had come. I was well on my way to being a writer. Goodbye garden world and hello Hollywood.

But things never felt right after the initial wave of excitement. I couldn't help but feel somewhat empty. I knew this wasn't my best writing, and that I hadn't put my head and heart fully in it. I had found a way to manipulate the system and it paid off.

The stories I wrote before and after that viral post were much better. I had a greater level of writer's pride after publishing them.

Even with that level of self-awareness, I still chased the need for another viral post. When I did that, the voices in my head made a dramatic appearance.

You know this isn't repeatable, right?

You realize this will change how you write moving forward?

What is your true motivation for writing, John?

Are you a "good writer" or are you learning to game the system?

Do I need to tabulate all of the time you've wasted fawning over and refreshing your stats?

Those voices were on to something. They needed to be addressed. Deep down I knew that answering those voices would allow me to evolve as a writer.

It didn't happen immediately, but as time went on I began to worry less about my stats and more about the quality and honesty of the writing. Those two sentiments were everything. If a post resonates with me and with readers and also happens to find its way to a large audience, that's great, but it's out of my control. I've learned just to write what I feel and not to cater to an audience.

I've learned to write deeper and not wider.

Writing isn't easy, and it isn't predictable. It's fun and it isn't fun. If I let it get inside my head too much, it messes with my writing process and ultimately erodes my passion behind it.

There's no need to define myself as a writer. I can be a garden writer one day and an agitated father writing about parenting the next day.

I just gotta be me.

I refuse to paint myself into a corner.

Let it happen naturally

When those voices do come back around:

Can I only make people giggle?

Am I incapable of deep thought?

Do I have a style and do I need to stay in my lane?

Do I validate my abilities by the numbers?

I simply acknowledge them, continue writing and move on.

> *Chew on this:* Hell yeah, the thrill of my post reaching so many was great. But it was also a reminder that there are no shortcuts when it comes to success. It's all about the effort and the heart; it takes time but the reward is often worth it.

CHAPTER 37

ALLISON IN OHIO

You have not lived today until you have done something for someone who can never repay you.

—John Bunyan

Writing can be a real mind f%^$.

We hit "Publish" and then we wait.

We wait for the "Likes."

We wait for the glowing comments.

We wait for heaps of praise to be bestowed upon us for our ability to tell a story, elicit emotions, or to make people LOL. Ideally we've done a little of all of these things.

But then there's silence.

No likes, no comments, and no views.

We debate deleting and moving on to the next. We debate our future as writers.

We question our judgment of what is good and what is crap.

And then you receive the following email during a particularly down time and realize maybe you're actually on to something. The ups and downs are so worth it.

Here is that exact email:

Subject: Where are you, dude?

"Where are you?" I click the link to ONG [Obsessive Neurotic Gardener, my blog name] today in my favorites bar, and nothing new since June 6. I log into Medium [Medium.com, where I also write] thinking, maybe the good word is here. And what do I see?.....a post about writer's block. Well great, I NEED gardening adventures and witty observations and whatever other crap you write about.

I don't say this in a selfish way. It's a compliment from me to you. I love your writing (the baseball stuff I can do without, but no one is perfect). If you decided to give it all up because it didn't make you happy, then good for you. I can appreciate that. Does it matter to you that I would approve?... Maybe. Maybe not. That is sort of the whole point, which I will get to in a minute.

I stumbled on the ONG blog while looking for advice for my zone 5a garden. You were close enough. I loved the way you styled your garden and I loved how honest you were about it; what worked and what didn't, how annoying the deer can be and, most importantly, you taught me that interesting foliage was the key to a beautiful and complete garden. I finally did enough research and feel confident in my choices and placements that I'm 99% certain I am going to be in love with my garden by next summer. (Evil Laughter yeah right, when is the garden ever finished?) The thing is, no matter what you write about YOU TELL YOUR TRUTH. It's what makes me connect to your writing. I do not want anything to do with kids, but when you wrote about losing the bedtime ritual with your daughter I cried like a baby at what that loss must feel like. When you make self-deprecating remarks, I'm one-upping you in my head.

The most important thing I found in your writing, in your truth, was that you do what satisfies you. You steal plant tags and tell the world about it. You seek out a private poop-room at work and live to tell the tale (Bee-Tee-Dubs...I do a version I call "Poop Chicken" at work). HERE IS THE POINT Whether you set out to or not, you have influenced me. I realized that I make other people way too much of a priority. Because you talk about taking walks with your weird dog, you helped me realize that I don't do enough of what makes me happy. You set writing exercise goals for yourself and I set the same goals. I have yet to write one single word. Oops. But it's okay, because I have started speaking up for myself when I have an opinion rather than thinking what I have to say doesn't matter. I have said "no" to things that I don't have time for without sacrificing time for myself. I have started looking for a new job so that I can have time to help in my community and to do the things I enjoy.

I'm sorry I never said this before: Thank you. Thank you. Thank you......thank you for every word you have written. It's not even about your garden or your family or your dog or your job or the fact that you feel you currently have nothing to say. It's just the fact that you said it, you admitted ALL of it, in the first place. I saw what you did. The topic didn't matter....granted, it's what drew me in. But I would read any of it because I find your way so genuine and from the heart.

So again I thank you and although I hope these are not your last installments, at least I gained something from what I experienced through your writing. And if you care about that, then great. And if you don't care, it's alright, because it's about doing what keeps you happy. Thank you. Thank you. Thank you.
Most Sincerely,
Allison in Ohio

I don't know anything more about "Allison in Ohio." I hadn't heard from her before this note, and I haven't heard from her since.

She has no idea what impact her words have had on me.

I can only hope to ever do the same for just one individual.

Thank you, "Allison in Ohio."

Whoever you are.

Chew on this: This note came at a time when I was questioning my worthiness as a writer. This got me back on my feet. It bears repeating: Keep doing "it," whatever "it" is for you.

CHAPTER 38

THE COLORING BOOK

There are no uninteresting things, only uninterested people.

—G.K. Chesterton

The temperature read 19 degrees Fahrenheit on the car's dashboard.

As I sat in my slow-to-warm vehicle, I questioned my destination over and over again. I could realistically back out and no one would be affected I could shut this car off, walk inside, and crawl back into my warm and inviting bed with my warm and inviting wife.

I like to set mini deadlines for myself throughout the day. It's a means to make a definitive decision and avoid the endless hemming and hawing.

As an example, it may be 7:02 a.m. on a November Saturday morning, and I need to decide if I'm going to drive over two hours to give a book talk to thirteen members of a garden club in Lackawaxen, Pennsylvania. The number of attendees could potentially be in the single digits. I'd be lucky to sell five books at a profit of 27 cents per book.

But I committed to doing it months before and the organizer had gone to great lengths to arrange this meeting.

So I set a deadline of 7:05 a.m. At that point, I would put the car in reverse and back out of the driveway or "this isn't worth it" would win out.

My deadline of 7:05 arrived and I drove off. No looking back at that point.

This will sound counterintuitive, but I listen to very loud and aggressive music to get myself in the right frame of mind for a talk or any form of public speaking. I also chug tons of black coffee. Not necessarily the recipe for a relaxing talk on perennials to an audience who have a mean age of 75, but it works for me.

So I'm enjoying head banging and the best means to extol the virtues of an *Amsonia* plant when Google Maps starts to get wacky. I'm about an hour into the drive and all had been okay up until this point. But then I'm told to make a left turn when a left turn was not an option. After a minute of confusion and recalculating, Google lady comes back and tells me very confidently to make a left on Simpson.

There is no "Simpson Street" but a left turn is approaching. So I decide to take said left and throw caution to the wind.

Said left took me down the wrong way on an off ramp for Rt. 80.

I freak, turn the music down, and back up blindly praying no one made as bad of a decision as I just made.

Luckily I navigated out of that disaster without issue and pulled to the side so Google could catch its breath.

Within minutes after that I was driving down a narrow road within a park. I made the assumption this was a creative means to get me back on track. The reality was it was yet another cruel Google joke as I was on a walking path, hence the demand to "turn left" without a road name identified.

Because I'm quick on my feet, I make the smart decision to drive across preserved land in order to hook up with real road again. There was no time for a mini deadline. If I were to get stuck in the damp earth funded by taxpayer money, I would abandon the car and take an Uber home.

I survived the trek and got to my destination with fewer than ten minutes before starting time.

If I had to estimate and round down, there were zero people there when I arrived. Just me and the host and a few people enjoying baked banana bread.

The projector I was promised was there, but it was still in its box, not yet opened.

I opened it and quickly realized no one in the audience would be able to see my presentation projected on the wall because the projection was the size of an open magazine.

I'd have to improvise.

I sat among the audience, all eleven of them.

As strange as the circumstances were and knowing that I'd be potentially losing their interest rather quickly, I still put on my bowler hat from '89 and went all Hardy on them.

I performed with joy.

I performed as if the room were full.

I held my laptop overhead and shared it with the

audience oscillating fan style.

Only three people fell asleep to the point of wheezing.

I did my best not to latch on to blank stares.

I finished my presentation and after a seven-second delay, received applause.

I sold seven books. Not a bad ratio of books sold to attendees. I'd done worse.

I chatted up a few die-hard gardeners and we shared lists of our favorite perennials. We planned a seed swap in spring.

I signed a book for one woman (always an odd undertaking) who turned out to be from the same hometown as I am (Midland Park, New Jersey, for those who skipped some of the early chapters). She even shared the same last name as my grandmother. We talked about street names, businesses, the hundred churches that existed in a town that is maybe three square miles, and all of the Dutch influences we grew up with. She was very kind, and we engaged in great plant conversation. She seemed to be the conservative type, the type of person where I would hold back on my cursing.

There were three of us left in the room: myself, hometown friend, and the host. The host was a fun woman who had a tattoo on the back of her neck and seemed to let the world simply roll off of her back.

She approached me as I was leaving and asked if I had "a good sense of humor." I replied with *"hells yeah"* and she told me to wait while she got a copy of the book she had just published.

The host returned with an adult coloring book entitled

All About Dick.

I thumbed through the book and enjoyed the drawings of all of the characters, all of whom were male genitalia come to life.

The host informed me the book was social commentary.

My fellow Midland Park'er was given one as well. She looked horrified, so I avoided her glances my way.

I thanked the host for the gift and promised to share it on social media. (I never did; is that bad?)

I got in my vehicle and placed the coloring book on the passenger seat. As I placed it down, I caught the name of the "author" for the first time.

It was Lalu Fauque; must be of French origin.

The trip was so worth it. I laughed the entire drive home. I shouted "Lalu Fauque" out the window.

I also realized that I had never felt more at ease with chaos then I did that morning. This worked for me. I want a lot more of it.

> ***Chew on this:*** I was so close to saying "no" to this experience. I'm glad that I didn't. Try to say "yes" more often than "no" even if "no" is easier.

CHAPTER 39

MY WIFE

Being deeply loved by someone gives you strength, while loving someone deeply gives you courage.

—Lao Tzu

When someone asks me how I met my wife, I have to pause and make a judgment call. Do I tell them the real story, or do I give them the watered-down version?

The real story is way more fun and detailed and kind of hilarious. The watered-down version allows me to get it over within 30 seconds. It's not always an easy call as I need some time to quickly evaluate my audience.

If I'm willing to embarrass myself, and we have some time to chat, you get the real story.

If it's a business function or my audience isn't into depravity, they get the vanilla version. I hate giving anyone the vanilla version because I hate being anything but 100 percent authentic. It pains me to water it down.

Here's the boring version in seven words: We met in college through mutual friends.

Here's the more exciting and real version in 257 words.

My cousin visited me at my school. We proceeded to

get drunk in the middle of the day. He had a friend who was at my same school and we looked her up on some directory. We attempted to call her on her dorm room "floor phone" (no one had phones in their dorm room and cellphones didn't really exist in 1990). My future wife just happened to walk by the floor phone and picked up the call. She agreed to sign in two degenerates so we could say "hi" to my cousin's friend. I obnoxiously opened a Bud Dry on the elevator ride. The friend wasn't around so we hung out with my future wife and her roommate. We were as annoying as you are now imagining but apparently not enough to chase us away. Later that night I hung upside down on a bicycle rack and attempted to eat potato chips. I kicked my shoe off of my foot and onto the roof of her dorm building. I told my future wife that my mom was going to kill me. I got my future wife's phone number and bragged to my floormates the next day only to realize that we had hatched a plan to someday commute to another college together so I could visit my friend and she could visit her boyfriend. I found my way back to my future wife's dorm room the next day and apologized for my behavior. We hung out the next weekend at a party. The rest is history.

Saying "the rest is history" is oversimplifying it.

I still remember her note to me on the whiteboard on my dorm room door that made me grin from ear to ear.

I remember bonding over our love of Def Leppard and Tesla.

I remember Valentine's Day in 1992.

I remember studying for a psychology exam together

at Washington Crossing Park in spring. There were no intentions to study.

I remember telling her "I love you" for the first time. It was in the laundry room of my dorm.

I remember skipping out on frat parties to eat Chinese food and listen to The Black Crowes in her dorm room.

I remember telling her I wanted to get married as I kicked away a rat right before we boarded the Staten Island Ferry on our way into New York City.

I remember our first trip together to New Orleans, our first chance to explore together. We almost died on a rickety boat in a bayou.

Looking back now, I really feel bad for my wife. She must have felt a massive wave of regret. I know that I would have considered reversing our decision. All signs pointed toward an uneasy and uncertain future.

When she saw me, and then the shutter, fall past that window and onto the hood of my car, she had to know that home ownership was going to be a challenge for the remainder of her life. If I couldn't hang a shutter, what would happen when more-complex house issues popped up?

To her credit, she stayed with me.

I don't mean "stay with me" as much as I mean "she accepted the journey." She accepts my shortcomings. She nudges me when I need to be nudged. She sincerely applauded me when I fixed the riding lawnmower on my own, even though it took me 14 hours to do it.

She picked up on my burgeoning love of gardening and pushed me to pursue it. She presented me with the world's greatest gardening gloves after hours of extensive research. She educated herself on the hottest gardening tools and presented them to me on Father's Day year after year. She sent me links to new garden centers. She suggested books. She fed my passion.

Never once has she questioned the boxes that arrive on a daily basis in spring. She knows that I try to hide newly purchased plants from the local nursery, but she remains quiet. She accepts the filthy backseat in my car and the mulch from my trunk that attaches itself to the grocery bags.

My wife left the very first comment on my very first blog post. As is her way, it was written simply but effectively. She reads everything I write and to her credit, doesn't blindly like it all. When she says, "That was a great post," I know that it was truly a great post.

Her feedback means more to me than anything. I trust her judgment unequivocally.

My wife was the content editor for this book. She has such a knack for it. She has an understanding of what readers want. I wrote this book with passion and vigor and the words just rolled off of my fingers and onto the keyboard.

But she is the one who helped me pull it all together. I hope to one day get to her to write for the world. I'm not exaggerating or feigning modesty when I say she is a far better writer than I am.

Chew on this: It's never fun to do it alone.

CHAPTER 40

MY WORK WIFE

It is more fun to talk with someone who doesn't use long, difficult words but rather short, easy words like "What about lunch?"

—A.A. Milne

I remember the day he started working in my department back in 2003. We were a rather stuffy corporate bunch back then and in walks this Bronx accent that stood out in the most awesome way possible. I wouldn't call it *coworker-love-at-first-sight*, but it was close.

Matt walked into my comfortably sized cubicle later that day and, being the diligent worker that I was, I found only a few seconds to greet him, catch his name, and then part ways. There were emails to return and urgent instant messages awaiting a response. We could exchange pleasantries at a more convenient time for me.

We interacted some those first few weeks but nothing of substance. I held off on passing judgment until we could get some quality one on one time. That is where I could put him under the microscope. He just needed to get the "one on one" date card.

Only then could I determine:

Was he a drinker of the corporate Kool-Aid?

Was he willing to listen and absorb rather than impart his wisdom?

Did he curse? (I like cursing.)

Did he like sports or The Real Housewives *series?*

Could he easily be distracted off the job at hand like me?

Was he funny enough?

We had our first date, our first meeting, about a month into his tenure. I think we were to discuss an upcoming website release and how we were going to write scripts for testing.

The meeting was scheduled for an hour and we had the conference room all to ourselves. I had my test plan, timeline, and a flip phone. I may have lit a candle; I can't remember.

We discussed testing for about 37 seconds. The remaining 59 minutes and 23 seconds were like a whirlwind.

You like the Mets too? Wow.

You collected baseball cards? Same here.

You know every line from The Sopranos? Stop already.

You obsess over yogurt varieties? Did you read my diary?

I kid you not; he gave me a bro hug when the meeting ended.

Swoon.

Fast-forward 15 years and Matt and I are inseparable. He is my work wife. We even had a commitment ceremony to profess our bromance to our cubemates. We finish each other's…sandwiches.

From the day we had that first meeting back in 2003,

we have been besties at work. We've never had even one fight. We've lived through the births of children, deaths in the family, and harrowing car rides along the nation's most terrifying road (check out "Clinton Road, NJ" on YouTube).

For visual purposes, imagine me as Vince Vaughn (prominent forehead and all) and Kevin James as Matt (except Matty B is funnier and has made better career choices). It's a near match as we've been told over and over again.

I grew up in the safe suburbs of New Jersey and Matt grew up on the streets of the Bronx in NYC.

I am Dutch/Polish and Matt is 100 percent Italian.

Matt grew up with some "connected" cohorts; I knew a kid who once threw a stink bomb in the bathroom in eighth grade.

I followed the preconceived path of high school, college, and safe corporate job. Matt graduated high school and then had bit acting parts in *A Bronx Tale* and *Bonfire of the Vanities*.

I am an awkward hugger and handshaker upon meeting/greeting you. Matt goes in for the hug and kiss with everyone.

Matt knows which cable channels could potentially be showing *The Exorcist* and stays away with fervor. I love me some horror.

Through all of those differences, we still work.

It's often said that men marry their mothers. I work-married my wife. They're both New York City-born Italians with a heart of gold, easily stressed, and an extreme fondness for all things '80s. Not to mention an unhealthy love of Bon Jovi, but only with Richie Sambora in tow.

Matt and I have had cubicles near each other, next to each other, and have even shared a cubicle over the years. We're back to sharing now, and I'm waiting for the day the teacher separates us for having too much fun together.

But our most memorable and cherished time spent together is at lunch. We go out to lunch together twice a week (due to schedules) and have been doing so for 14 years. Multiply 49 (52 weeks minus vacation) x 2 x 15 and you get, well, a really large number of lunches together.

Ninety-nine percent of those lunches have been spent at Wegmans, a supermarket/kicked up food court. We started a blog together about our lunches there ("Two Guys at Lunch"). We walk around the aisles after lunch and look at food labels together. We debate the best yogurts. We walk in giant circles around the store to increase the step count on our collective Fitbit devices. We talk life.

I know that our coworkers are well aware of our bromance. They see us leave for lunch every day, weather be damned, laughing and without a care in the world. They see us return from lunch with Wegmans bags in hand, usually a few protein bars carefully selected after reviewing each and every one on the shelf. They see us head down to the cafeteria at three each afternoon for coffee and biscotti.

They can laugh if they want. I don't care what they

think.

We are the best of friends and that makes the work day manageable. If one of us is down, the other is there for support. I've never laughed harder in my life than when we're hanging. We could pull off a killer stand-up act based on conference call observations. We bounce half-assed business ideas off each other. We do deep when it's needed.

As we reach the twilight of our corporate careers, I can only hope we have more lunches and more laughs. We'll never mature, and I'm proud of that. I'm one lucky dude to have befriended Matty B. The term "bromance" has worn thin and "broworker" doesn't really capture it.

I'll just stick with friend, a kick-ass friend.

> ***Chew on this:*** Jim Rohn, the famous entrepreneur and author once said, "We are the average of the five people we spend the most time with." Matt falls into that group of five and so does my wife. That's a great start. Who are your five?

CHAPTER 41

RUNNING OUT OF TIME

Garden as though you will live forever.

—William Kent

What I've enjoyed presenting to my blog readers over the years is a peek into my own garden and what I'm doing, be it educational or smart or just plain dumb.

I've also enjoyed sharing the emotions that come with hardcore gardening because yes, gardening is an emotional undertaking.

There is anger when big plans fall apart over the winter.

There is frustration when there is no answer as to why that stupid perennial still won't bloom after three years in the ground.

There is elation on those days when it all seems to come together.

There is indifference when you get tired and start to question whether or not it's all worth it.

All of those emotions often occur within the same day.

I've also taken to sharing the evolution not only of the garden as a whole, but also that of specific plants. When I can, I like to capture plants in their infancy and then document their growth in subsequent years. I also enjoy sharing a plant's ever-changing look and feel from season to season.

With that information in hand, it helps when deciding whether or not to purchase said plant and how it fits into your overarching garden vision.

A few years back my wife and I were enjoying one of our typical romantic soirees; we were both on our devices on separate couches while the kids watched *Family Feud* and the dog jumped from couch to couch trying to determine which was more comfortable and which adopted parent would offer up more attention. (P.S., my wife wins every time.)

After one of the many Steve Harvey lines of *"Survey says?"* my wife handed me her iPad to show me a blog she had been reading. The author of the blog, her husband, and their young children were picking apples from a tree while skipping and smiling and enjoying life to the fullest.

A f'n Hallmark moment.

The perfect life presented as only a blogger can.

The real intention was for me to see that the apple tree was producing four different fruits on one tree. She had never seen that before and admittedly, neither had this so-called expert gardener.

I handed the iPad back to my wife with the intention of then researching this fascinating apple tree to see if it was legitimate.

But I couldn't shake the photo.

Yes, I realized it was a staged pic and the kids more than likely were fooled into giving a shit for sake of their mom's blog, but it still grabbed my attention for a number of reasons.

How did my own children get so old, so fast, and were they already beyond the age of wanting to really hang with us?

Could we legitimately pull off this type of scene ourselves?

How much longer do we actually have in our current home knowing we'd like to move south in the future because we both hate the cold with a passion; maybe nine to ten years?

How does that factor into what I still plant here knowing our rough timeline?

Why haven't I tried growing an apple tree before?

It was all about the fear of time.

That night I went to the Stark Brothers website determined to purchase an apple tree or two. I still had time to nurse these trees to the point of giving fruit before my daughter entered high school. Poorly draining clay soil be damned; I'd figure it out somehow.

Within ten minutes I had purchased three trees:

'Honeycrisp'

'Red Rome Beauty Apple' (as a pollinator for the 'Honeycrisp')

'4 on 1 Antique Apple' (yes, similar to what we had seen in the blog post)

Time was of the essence and I could not deal with the regret of not having at least tried to grow apple trees. Too spontaneous? One could argue that, but I got caught up in the moment and allowed the fear of running out of time to get the best of me.

I planted the three bareroot trees in early spring that year. It was a bit cold and windy, and really wet, but I feared not getting these in the ground soon enough.

After digging the holes and planting, I tried my best to ignore the reminders of how wet the soil stays with our high water table.

Too late, I was all in.

And determined to make it work.

Time was running out.

I even mapped out a plan to massively expand an existing garden bed off my deck that would include two of the apple trees and a nearby river birch. It would be a small seating area with some large pots since I didn't want to mess with the roots of the three trees.

My emotions got the best of me here and I'm glad that they did.

The future with these trees should be fun, frustrating, scary, and annoying.

I love the fact that gardening is something that we can do for life. I love that, in theory, what we plant can remain there well after we're gone.

Yet as I get older and the kids get older, I've found myself in a bit of a panic. I often feel like I'm running out of time. I don't want to ever stop having a catch or shooting hoops with my son. I don't want my daughter to ever stop believing in Santa Claus. I want to take walks with my wife while we still can without complaining about lower back pain.

I want to get as much in the ground as I possibly can before we move on. That became the ultimate motivation for planting those apple trees. I so fear looking back and saying that I regretted not trying.

To counter that fear I remind myself that another family may move in here and they may be able to enjoy the trees we planted. They, too, can enjoy all of the swaying grasses in fall and winter. It doesn't have to end with us.

Just knowing someone else will continue to tend to the garden I built from scratch is deeply rewarding.

Or if they tear it all down and add more lawn I'll be physically ill.

Oh, how we gardeners suffer.

You want to know how I best deal with this fear of time running out?

I write.

I write about my garden.

I write about my family.

I write about time running out.

I write about my family and the garden.

I write about time running out in my garden with my family.

They all play off of one another and they all inspire writing that carries a deeper meaning beyond just plants.

Chew on this: Don't be held hostage by your age or time. You're never too old to pursue what you love. Don't leave room for regret. You'll never regret failing but you will regret not trying.

CHAPTER 42

WALK

Everywhere is walking distance if you have the time.

— Steven Wright

It's 11:03 p.m. and if I have to estimate, it's about 22 degrees Fahrenheit outside.

I step into my indestructible four-year-old flip-flops, socks still on. You know the next required move; wiggle your feet while at the same time pushing with a decent amount of force so the single flip-flop strap moves and ultimately rests comfortably between the big toe and the toe just to the right or to the left of the big guy. I don't think that toe has an official name.

I place my Oakland Raiders winter hat, pom-pom and all, atop my sizable head.

I pull my hoodie's hood over the hat for the ultimate in cold and wind protection.

I hook the leash onto the dog's collar before putting on my gloves. If I put the gloves on first it's impossible to grasp the hook thingy on the leash and the dog gets very impatient. She leaps at the door knob as if to say,

"What the hell would you do, human, if someone blocked you for like a minute and a half right when your need to urinate was at its peak?"

I open the front door, allow myself to be temporarily blinded by the projected-onto-the-house Christmas lights from the front lawn, grab a railing anticipating the dog pulling me with angry fervor, and slowly descend the front steps.

Yes, we are cheating by using *those* lights rather than going through the age-old ritual of taking hours to painfully hang lights on the gutters or the railings or the shrubbery knowing that the final results will never meet expectations.

I don't care and neither do the kids. That's a win-win.

While the dog pees, I scan my surroundings for ne'er-do-wells. We live in the middle of nowhere without street lights and everyone else who lives on the street is asleep in their comfy beds with their comfy comforters and duvet covers.

It's just me and the elements, and I need to know what I'm up against. If I sense a coyote or hobo is present, we will quickly turn around and head back inside to safety and warmth.

On this night all appears okay, so we proceed with our walk.

Oh, how I cherish these walks.

I kill for those long late-night walks with the dog. While they started as an obvious means to get the dog outside and to give her exercise, I think they now benefit me more than her.

And it's not really about the exercise for me. I am a runner (ahem) and manage to fit in a few runs per week. These walks just supplement the exercise I'm already getting.

Okay, that's not totally true. I'm a Fitbit fanatic, and have been tracking my every step for three years now. I have no choice but to get 11,000 steps per day. That is the minimum or the accepted floor. The ceiling sits around 16,000. I take every possible long-cut to up my step totals.

I park in the far right back of the parking lot at work and then walk to the left front to enter the building. That's a horrible description on my part but you get the point.

I abhor elevators.

I volunteer at home to get anything that is either in the basement or in the attic or in the car outside.

I walk in circles when I'm bored.

The walk with the dog results in anywhere from 1,500 to 2,000 steps. I factor that into my projected steps total at the beginning of each day.

So my bad, I take the walk for the exercise as well.

But more than that, nothing aids clearing the mind, promoting creative thinking, and reducing anxiety like a simple freaking walk.

I can easily talk myself off of panic highway with one of those late-night walks.

I dreamt up the concept of this book while walking the hallways at work.

I physically can't maintain a high anxiety level while moving.

My wife and I have made many important adult decisions while walking.

Why did it take so long to discover this? I don't know.

Don't punch me, but I always considered a walk to just be a slower run. Why wouldn't I just push myself to run where the benefits would be exponentially increased from just walking? I'm still young enough *not* to be one of those people who walk every night for their exercise. I am not that guy who walks the mall before it opens.

But you know what you can't do when running? Think.

You know what else you can't do while running? Enjoy the moment.

I've never had a creative thought while running. But I have had one post-run, while walking back into the house.

I'm now addicted to walking.

I expect a new and brilliant idea after every walk. If I could ever figure out a way to write while walking, well, the sky would be the limit. I would blow your mind with my while-walking words.

There are three distinct "walks" that are part of my repertoire most days. Each requires a different skill set. Each has its own quirks to contend with. Each carries different benefits, and each is crucial to my spiritual and creative awakening.

They are as follows:

The walk at work

Biggest benefit: Walk off work-induced stress within minutes. Put that God-awful conference call in the rearview.

Biggest drawback: Coworkers observing you walking without an apparent destination. Being branded as that weirdo. Walking with fancy shoes on can hurt after a while.

Go-to move: Never walk the same path twice. Pretend to be seeking a conference room or a trip to the bathroom or cafeteria. Never glance at the Fitbit device on your wrist.

The walk with my wife

Biggest benefit: Spouse bonding. Escape from the kids. Adulting. Life's toughest choices and decisions are made easier while in motion and slightly out of breath.

Biggest drawback: Returning to reality post-walk.

Go-to move: A location with as few people as possible and with as few distractions as possible so conversation can be locked in without distraction. Don't try to grab your wife's hand while walking. That is apparently very lame.

The late-night walk with the dog

Biggest benefit: The dog gets outside. The human gets outside. The danger of being attacked by a rabid raccoon or the stray bullet from a local hunter is invigorating. I value the glance back at the house where all the people I care most about are safe and secure inside.

Biggest drawback: The cold. The heat. The coyotes. The in-between-the-toes blisters from insisting on wearing flip-flops out of sheer laziness.

Go-to move: Three loops covering our street and the one running perpendicular to our street. Desperately being dragged by your unusually strong 25-pound mutt who chases every blowing leaf like it's a scurrying mouse.

The pleasure and benefits I've received from a simple walk pushed me to pursue mindfulness practices. I've been meditating for a year now and while I can't quite quantify the benefits as I'm still a beginner, I know this is leading me down a path I like a whole lot.

I've been writing "morning pages" for months now, which is similar to journaling. I write (yes, physically write with a pen) all of my thoughts down on paper as a means to clear my head in the morning. It then allows me to go about my day with a greater focus and it definitely aids my clarity of writing.

> ***Chew on this:*** Wherever you do your best thinking, in the car, in the shower, or on your daily walk with the dog, allow your mind to wander and do your best to log all of your good ideas.

CHAPTER 43

THE JOURNEY

It is good to have an end to journey toward; but it is the journey that matters, in the end.

—Ursula K. Le Guin

I have an infinite amount of patience like 98.7 percent of the time. It was blessed upon me at birth. It may be my greatest asset (or it's 1A with 1B being my inability to smell, which makes puppy feces clean-up or a 2 a.m. puke clean-up a task I can more easily manage than others). I like to think I've had a calming influence on most with whom I've interacted over the course of my time on this planet.

But I go batshit crazy when it comes to tying things, or securing things with straps, or doing anything with ropes.

A Boy Scout I am not.

The night before we headed out on our longest-to-date family road trip, I took on the responsibility of figuring out how to use our recently purchased dog harness/seat belt. I was in favor of tossing the dog in the trunk like I used to hang with my sisters in the family station wagon as kids of the '70s and '80s.

But my wife informed me we needed to be more

concerned about Mia's safety.

Mia, our rescue mutt, looks like the perfect mix of a Gremlin, the Hamburglar, and an Ethiopian wolf. Seriously, Google all three, and you'll know I'm right.

She's cute in a "What exactly is she?" kind of way.

I couldn't figure out the harness. I watched the instructional YouTube video. I carefully read through the instructions. I must have heard or read the phrase "Simply place the buckle" 112 times, and each time I lost it. Stop insulting me with your "simply." Nothing is simple for me.

My wife and daughter eventually figured it out because they are female and smarter, and we would crash and burn without them.

At 6:20 a.m. we were all in the car and ready for lots of hours together in a tiny tubelike structure. The dog was perfectly secured between the two kids in the back seat. They were all asleep by 6:33.

It was an adorable scene but I was also annoyed. These three have it so easy. Wake up, grab a blanket, walk thirty feet to the car, and collapse. They don't have a reminder list. They don't have to stay awake and aware. They don't have to stress over tying things.

I drove the entire trip. My wife had no choice. I'd like to say it's a manly/protector type deal and it is, but it's also more sinister than that. I need her not driving. I need her as navigator, planner, and captain of the ship. She owns the GPS and route changes on the fly. She owns online grocery shopping for the following week. She owns Yelp factoids for restaurants at our destination.

In other words, she owns everything.

I can then just concentrate on nothing but driving carefully.

The music we played on this trip was epic. There was enough Sirius XM Hits 1 for my Top 40-loving daughter to sate her pop appetite with the remainder of the tunes breaking down as follows:

20 percent—**"Hair Nation"**—I thought that Hair Metal love was more nostalgia than an appreciation of the long-haired musicianship, but I say Great White, Tesla, and Whitesnake still hold up.

10 percent—**"80s on 8", "Alt Nation," "The Highway"** (wife's choice), and maybe eight other stations—we are impatient and have to both agree before a choice is made.

70 percent—**"Yacht Rock Radio"**—MIND BLOWN. This station has the greatest collection of songs I thought I hated, but now realize I madly love. A few observations after consuming:

- Michael McDonald sang back-up vocals on 87 percent of the songs from the late '70s to early '80s.
- Ambrosia is sorely underrated.
- I was oddly moved by Kenny Loggins's "This Is It."
- Hearing Christopher Cross didn't make me vomit; instead, it made me long to see the movie *Arthur* again.
- I may have since visited the Wikipedia pages of Orleans, Robbie Dupree, and Gerry Rafferty.
- Speaking of Mr. Rafferty, "Baker Street" is my childhood. Love. Heart emoji.

I don't remember exactly when we agreed to do it, but

my wife and I are now comfortable cursing in front of the kids. They're still not allowed to partake in front of us at least. I'm cool with them throwing the occasional f-bomb as an angry outlet. There's a power in that word that exceeds all others and, if used properly, it can be a great tool for anger management.

When you are stuck in traffic for 90 minutes straight in Nowhere, Virginia, desperate for lunch and in awe of the ETA Google Maps is informing you, you have to do something to survive.

I chose imitations to break the monotony: imitations in various accents with a plethora of curse words. Good dad moment it was not. But I killed with my audience. I did Southern accent, I did Mid-Atlantic accent, I did snobby '80s accent, and I did the accent of specific people we know who shall remain nameless.

I can name ten road trips off the top of my head that were awful. Some were as little as an hour in duration. The moments when jumping out of a moving car seems like a viable option. Moments when you hear yourself say things like, "Stop putting your gum on your sister's ear" or "If you kick my seat one more time, I'll cut you." Once you arrive at your destination, it takes a good hour to recover.

This one was not one of those times. This one was special while it was happening. We all felt it. No drama, no screaming, very little complaining, and a ton of laughs.

My son has become mature and witty and knowledgeable on any topic one could dream up. I could talk with him for days.

My daughter is a dreamer, looking at all moments as an opportunity to have fun. She would want to play UNO while in the ocean. And really mean it.

My wife and I shared more than one glance at each other that said, *"We kind of nailed it."*

At the time, my son was 15 and my daughter was 12. I don't know how many more trips there will be where they are at least semi-interested in hanging with us. While I don't miss the back-seat shenanigans and the "he/she did it," I crave having them securely under our control in the car. I still see those little kid faces. I still remember when their car seats faced away from us, and we had to put a mirror on the back seat to be able to see them and to make sure they weren't choking.

I'm not ready for driving lessons. I'm not ready for hormones. I'm not ready to witness their heartbreaks. I'm not ready for college visits.

Heavy metaphor warning in case you didn't already see it:

The beauty is in the journey.

The beauty is in getting there.

The vacation ended up being just okay. There were some great memories and good times. But the trip to and from our destination was the most memorable. We still talk about it to this day. Just the five of us trapped in a car for 25-plus hours in total and nary a complaint.

The build-up and inevitable delay getting there allowed

us all to display our comedic chops.

The longer journey home was a chance to rehash memories with mom and dad coveting the fact that there were no distractions other than the hum of the car.

As a gardener I've come to embrace the struggles and triumphs that have come my way. I never want to be "done" designing my garden. I want it to be difficult until the day I die. I love walking outside in the morning, not sure what I'm going to discover. The process and the journey are everything, not the end results.

As a writer, we cherish positive feedback. We want to know that people enjoy what we put out into the world. I want you to like this book, and I want you to tell your friends.

But I've learned in real time, how much I've enjoyed the struggle in how to package it all for you. I've loved erasing entire pieces and mentally writing new chapters while driving in the car. I cherish the memories I've recovered.

It's the journey, man. It's the journey.

> **Chew on this:** I want to write for a living. That is my goal. But I'm doing my best to make sure I enjoy myself along the way. I'm embracing the highs and the lows as part of this journey. I encourage you to do the same.

CHAPTER 44

DAD

Death ends a life, not a relationship.

—Mitch Albom

Seeing that pastry sitting on the kitchen counter made us all laugh uncontrollably; it was so typical of him.

Laughter never felt so good and so wrong.

How do we get to do this after the brutal gut punch of the night before?

Sixteen hours earlier we had learned that my father-in-law had died in his apartment. He hadn't responded to our phone calls and texts from the prior two days. We all had a bad feeling and the dread continued to build until our worst fears were realized.

The 45-minute drive to his apartment was torture. The text from his girlfriend had said it all:

"Come now."

We hit every red light. We all took turns breaking down. We all attempted to create an alternative ending that we knew wasn't possible.

The summer air never felt thicker or more ominous.

When we arrived at the scene it was straight out of a movie. The parking lot was filled with police officers with grim faces. Onlookers gathered at the restaurant next door. When the lead officer extended his condolences to us, my wife threw up in the bushes.

We had to decide between cremation and a burial in five minutes.

We had to pick a location for the memorial service and we chose the most convenient for those who would have to travel. Was that the right thing to do?

We had to call the kids and tell them grandpa had died. Their cries still haunt us to this day.

He was only 68 and had signed for the purchase of a beach house at the Jersey Shore two days prior.

He had retired months earlier. We attended the surprise celebration, and there is nothing more painful now than seeing him light up when he realized we were there.

He fought his way back from financial ruin during the past ten years.

He promised my daughter that she could kayak right from his backyard.

He made it.

And then he fucking didn't.

It was the cruelest of cruel jokes. There was no way this could be happening. If there is a Lord above, well, there must not be.

None of us wanted to see his body. There was no way that was going to be the lasting memory. We preferred the smile he wore as we toured the new house with him a week earlier. We preferred the excitement he exuded as he took us to Stewart's on the canal for ice cream. We preferred his determined face as he surveyed his soon-to-be property and took measurements for a future project.

The morning after he died we made the trek back to his apartment. It was brutal. It still looked like a scene from a movie, a scene calling for nothing but normalcy.

His dinner bowl was still on the dining room table, partially full.

There was a pen resting on a mortgage form.

A blood pressure machine sat innocently next to his laptop.

A typical weeknight scene and he was ripped right from it. We refuse to ponder if he knew what was coming.

Upon closer inspection, we found the pastry. He legendarily loved his pastries and often tried to hide them. We once found a bear claw in his jacket pocket and laughed about it for hours.

This felt appropriate, hilarious, and bitterly sad.

We had to clear out his apartment within two weeks so the next renter could be secured. Life goes on.

For two weeks we had to make decisions of keep versus garbage, and we were in no state to do that. We invaded his privacy with reckless abandon. We laughed like mad as we unearthed forgotten memories. We cried realizing he had probably been saving all the gift cards we'd given him for the past few years to help furnish his new retirement home.

As time goes on the timing of his death still feels cruel yet poetic. He did make it. He fought through adversity for two decades to get to this point. He signed the papers and with that it was mission truly accomplished.

He doesn't get to live out that last phase of his life and that will always hurt.

This is why I convinced myself to write and publish this book now. I have no idea how it will all turn out and if anyone will like it, let alone read it.

I didn't want to wait any longer to find out.

> **Chew on this:** Whatever it is you want to do, please start it now.

WANT MORE?

Join John's email list at
www.obsessiveneuroticgardener.com

Follow John on twitter @jmarkowski0

Follow John on Instagram @jmarkowski0

CPSIA information can be obtained
at www.ICGtesting.com
Printed in the USA
BVHW04*2049220518
517051BV00001B/3/P

9 780692 107676